Blessin

52 DEVOTIONS FROM THE PSALMS

Joan Moss relies on Scripture to bring hope to mothers suffering the relentless grief of losing a child.... Her freeing and strengthening devotional covers the many facets of grief she has personally experienced—despair, anger, guilt, loneliness and more. Joan knows first hand that only God can heal us, and he is more than willing. Let her walk you into the loving and merciful words of Jesus with each chapter. She has written an essential, comprehensive and beautiful book.

—*Lara Stark, Author of Bridal Veil Fireweed,*
The Tale of the Woodswalker and Calla Lily Dreams

Grief... is a difficult and often surprising experience. One surprise may be (its) wide variety of emotions. This devotional is a... guide to the comforting relevance of the Psalms as messages of reassurance that God is with us.

—*Carolyn Havlen, Facilitator at GriefShare, New Mexico*

As a bereaved mother... this book would have been helpful as I went through so many emotions, especially in the first year.

—*Roberta Swanhart, Darren's mom, New Mexico*

This book invites itself to be given as a gift to women who need its message of hope.

—*Teena Marcus, Women's Book Study Leader, Hope Church,*
New Mexico

I lost my 27-year-old daughter over thirty years ago. The Lord has healed a lot of my pain. Joan's book still touched me very deeply. As a Biblical counselor and senior pastor, I see this as a good resource which I highly recommend.

—*Rev. Patricia H. Bergsland, retired pastor*
and mother of Ann Scott, New York

Blessings for a Grieving Mother

52 DEVOTIONS FROM THE PSALMS

Joan Moss

All for Him!
Joan Moss
2021

Blessings for a Grieving Mother
52 DEVOTIONS FROM THE PSALMS
Joan Moss

ISBN: 9781707880829
Imprint: Independently published

Dedication

This book is dedicated to all children who left too soon . . . including

Matthew Kelch ♣ Gary Ritenburg ♣ David Harris
M.O. Phillips ♣ Darren Haas ♣ Melanie Falcon
Ann Scott McCormick ♣ Matthew Gurule ♣ Michael Davenport
Cathy Johnson ♣ Shirley Kozlowski ♣ David Cotter
Robin Weber ♣ Sara Ironside

Also

_____

_____

_____

Contents

Foreword

Joan's book, *Blessings for a Grieving Mother*, is sure to find a place with any Christian mother who has had a child (or perhaps more than one) succumb to a disease or other catastrophe. Joan writes comforting thoughts based on her own experience and grounded in scripture.

I am a mother who had to say goodbye to my four-year-old daughter much too soon, and I relate to much of what Joan describes about the grief involved. It is an upheaval of what we believe about nature—to have a child predecease the parent goes against our heart's expectation and is as devastating a loss as we can imagine. I am also a licensed grief counselor in both New Mexico and Oregon, and as a professional counselor, I have devoted many years of my life listening to heartbreaking stories of bereaved parents.

It will be good to have several copies of Joan's book on hand to give to grieving mothers. She writes from experience and from her Christian heart.

—*Mary A. Johnson, Ph.D.*

Licensed Grief Counselor and bereaved parent
Albuquerque, New Mexico

Introduction

Be merciful to me, LORD, for I am in distress;
my eyes grow weak with sorrow, my soul and body with grief.
My life is consumed by anguish and my years by groaning;
my strength fails because of my affliction, and my bones grow weak.
PSALM 31:9-10

I am a grieving mother.
I can't pray...
> but God gives me words

My tears won't stop...
> but God is collecting them

I can't eat...
> but God fills me

I hate myself...
> but God loves me

I'm lost...
> but God knows the way

My heart is crushed...
> but God is my healer

My mind is at war...
> but God brings peace

I can't function...
> but God is working in me

I'm so alone...
> but God sends his Spirit

I'm angry...
> but God understands

The pain won't stop...
> but God comforts me

I don't know how to do this...
> but God does

I can't remember beauty...
> but God's creation reminds me

I'm so scared...
> but God protects me

2

I'm broken...
> but God is restoring me

My foundations are shaking...
> but God is in control

I can't... I can't... I can't...
> but God can.

You are a mother grieving for your child, and God, in his great love, has something surprising to tell you. He wants you to know that your exceptional grief is a crown of jewels made up of many facets. This is grief from God's point of view. As you open your heart to these devotions, the Psalms display the rubies, diamonds and emeralds that glitter in this crown. They are symbols of royalty—of kinship with the King. They are God's blessings for mothers who grieve. But first he tells us that he understands our distress and anguish. He hears our groans. He knows, because he's been there. Listen...

"This will hurt her, I know," God says. "But because I cherish her and her child, I am allowing this in her life. Her trial will be long and hard and many times she will have to look away, as I did when my Son's earthly life ended. She will know my pain and I will know hers. I'll stay with her and hold her when she cries, and in this special relationship—this sharing of great pain—she'll find the blessings I chose for her at creation. Looking into eternity, I see her light being passed from one to another, shining so others can see. She will know this way of grief is a special way Home."

"What?" you cry, "There are no blessings in this grief—only suffering and loneliness—and a wild array of other terrifying emotions! How can I see any good in life when I've been ambushed by this hideous tragedy, the loss of my child? I shrink from it, yet clutch it as a remnant because I have nothing left. I fell down Alice's rabbit hole and it's deep and empty. Evil took my child and left me helpless, with this monster trailing me around, this grief. I hate it, yet I love it. It's my only identity, a terrible badge of misery. And I'm not alone. There are many of us whose children left and we were never ready to let them go."

And God understands. He knows that our grief is profound because this loss defies the natural order. Our maternal souls have been so violently attacked that we will never be the same. A vital part of us left with our child, and God understands this, because he gifted us in a secret, miraculous way with the giving and receiving of this baby. He recorded that moment in the prayer of our child. "For you created my inmost being; you knit me together in my mother's womb. I praise you because I am fearfully and wonderfully made; your works are wonderful, I know that full well" (Psalm 139:13-14). The knitting of a child in a mother's womb is the most sacred of all events between God and humans. Perhaps that's why Jesus chose this way to enter the world.

My life feels dark because two of my daughters left me in the space of two years, snatched by the demon, cancer. I fumble, trying to find the light, and with the merciful help of the Holy Spirit, I'm finding Jesus. He's helped me realize that we mothers who are suffering this grief, as his mother did, are blessed. The sad truth is, there's no other way to discover what this journey will teach us. It's a mystery that defies reason, so I don't question why God chose some of us for these unsought blessings. They're the roads he has laid out for us to honor him and ourselves in ways we could never have imagined. In the years since my girls left, I've endured terrible pain. "But God..." I say, at least twenty times a day, as in "I'm going through pure hell right now... but God is here and he knows." His presence with us, especially now, is a blessing. Through the sweetness of his Spirit, I'm learning that even though we sit in darkness, he is creating something beautiful of our lives.

I share your grief and I embrace you. Looking into your eyes, I see my pain reflected. We endure the same loss and ask the same questions and cry the same tears. We miss our children with every breath. Ours is a fragile sisterhood and we need each other. So I come as a friend, and together we discover a bit of how God works, and his blessings. To be blessed is to be favored by God, with gifts designed by him for this particular grief. They are tools we can use to hack our way out of this terrifying jungle and finally emerge on a sunlit mountaintop where the rainbow rests. It seems impossible, I know, but God will explain. He, unlike many others in our lives, understands our pain. Because he gave up his only Son for us, he's there with comfort and strength when we turn to him.

In the early days of grief, as I half-heartedly leafed through my Bible, these phrases from the Psalms were hurled out to me like a lifeline: "The LORD is my shepherd, I lack nothing"... "He has crowned me with loving-kindness and tender mercies"... "You are my rock." The Psalms became beautiful channels for my survival. For example, Psalm 10:14 says: "But you, God, see the trouble of the afflicted; you consider their grief and take it in hand. The victims commit themselves to you..." Here God asks that we commit ourselves to him in this storm. He comes alongside and encourages, comforts, and teaches us, the afflicted. We find that the Psalms are giant lighthouses, assuring that we can trust God in the dark.

These devotions reveal how God blesses the many aspects of a mother's grief. Because this journey is different for every mother, it has no set pattern or timing. Each phase can flow into another as a gentle stream or a violent hurricane. Certain phases may return many times and others may never show up. So grief takes no hard and fast route, but I pray you will be comforted in knowing that you are not traveling alone. Most importantly, we are assured that by staying close to God while doing the work of grief, we will discover special meaning in our loss, immense "knowing" of him and his mysteries—and best of all, the safe harbor of his blessings.

P.S. Please be reminded that these 52 devotions are not to be considered a "course" with specific steps to follow. They can be used in any order and time frame you wish. Some readers may browse the contents for a relevant theme, while others might prefer a weekly routine which completes the book in a year. Let your heart choose the rate and sequence of your study. Hold these blessings close as you savor and pray over the words. For a deeper experience, use the Bible to expand on each psalm, and keep a journal of your thoughts, concerns and discoveries as you make this journey with Jesus.

1

Shock

Fear and trembling have beset me;
horror has overwhelmed me.
PSALM 55:5

It was four in the morning. The hospice nurse touched my
shoulder and whispered, "Joan, she's gone." I bolted up from
the cot. "Gone where?" my mind cried, unbelieving. "How
could she go without me?" Reeling to Robin's bed, I looked
and I knew. Her face was turned toward the window, as if
drawn by an invisible image. Her Beloved had come for her;
she was gone. Then a black curtain fell down around me.

We may not remember those days of raw grief when we
spent most of our time wondering what happened to us. This
is severe distress and nothing makes sense. Even crying seems
hollow and empty. All our emotions are unfamiliar, and none of
them come close to expressing this new reality that's been thrust
upon us. Instead, we sit staring, or throw ourselves into frenzied
preparations. Or both. This is the horror of hearing that our
child has left and will never return to this earth. Our life has
changed forever and we're sure God has abandoned us. We may
cry over and over, "Where are you?" We're overwhelmed and
lost in a confused daze. We're in shock.

The blessing of this initial stage is that shock and denial
protect us from facing a reality that is too horrible to grasp.
They are coping skills to help us survive the tragedy. Our
minds, hearts and spirits are unable to accept that our children
are gone. So we watch for them to show up, or we escape
by sleeping around the clock, often aided by a sedative. We
may go about our normal routine as if in a dream, seemingly
unaware of what has happened. This dense fog is God's way of
letting in only what we can handle. Our minds need time to
absorb the unthinkable, and shock may linger for many weeks.
Then there's a shift and we realize that God is easing us into
a new place—like gently lowering us into a tub of something

new and awful. All the feelings we were denying begin to surface. He knows we're frightened, and like a good Father, he holds us close and whispers our name. And that's where he stays, because as the shock lifts, we begin to drown, and we're terrified.

My God, my God, why have you forsaken me? I can't do this alone. What has happened? Why can't I think? Where are you? I'm trying to trust, to breathe. But it's so dark and I need your help. Where is my child?

After the initial shock, is your mind still denying certain aspects of what has happened? Do you need help releasing full expression of your grief? For example, some mothers have kept their home arranged as if their child would be returning. This may be helpful for a while, but long-term denial can hinder healing.

2

Fear

Save me, O God, for the waters have come up to my neck.
I sink in the miry depths, where there is no foothold.
I have come into the deep waters; the floods engulf me.
PSALM 69:1-2

They will have no fear of bad news;
their hearts are steadfast, trusting in the LORD.
Their hearts are secure, they will have no fear;
in the end they will look in triumph on their foes.
PSALM 112:7-8

Oh no, this is so real! We are engulfed by rising water and sinking in mud where there's no footing! These terrors hint at the degree of fear we face as the initial shock wears off. Now reality is beginning to set in, and we're sure to drown in this grief. We fear facing life without our children because they are so closely tied to our identity of motherhood. One of our basic foundations has crumbled and we're not sure we can survive. We also fear the possibility of more bad news in the future. We have lost all confidence, trust and the ability to cope. Evil has flooded our lives and threatens to drown us. Where can we turn? We are like the disciples in the storm-tossed boat who called out to Jesus and were spared (Matthew 14:22-31). So that's what we do, and that's where we find the blessing. Fear has caused us to depend on God, which leads to the next step. As his power begins to calm the storm, our grateful hearts realize more than ever who he is and how much we need him.

In the Bible, this realization is called "fear of God," or seeing him as all-knowing and all-powerful. In a more helpful description, we do not cower in fear but embrace him with reverence and awe. We find the one who is our anchor, who will keep us safe in this storm and hold us close.

While fear in early grief is normal, we must fight despair. Despair says, "I give up, I can't live, I'm lost forever." Those are lies of Satan, the father of lies. Instead, we turn away and place ourselves in the presence of Jesus. There we can face our fears and ask for help. We focus on him, talk to him, lean on him every day, becoming Psalm 112 people—learning to trust in the LORD.

This facing of fear may also include time with a compassionate friend who won't put up with fake bravery. This is one who asks "How are you doing?" and knows better when you answer, "I'm fine." Hidden emotions can backfire and turn inward, causing ulcers, panic attacks and other problems. With God we can express our fears honestly, and he will send someone to listen.

In grief, we have become very fragile and may continue to be plagued by small fears—as when we're bumped or startled or drop things, or especially when driving in traffic. So even though we've turned to God, we may have to wait a while for relief, because God often gives his blessings gradually. This is so we can practice dependence on him and trust in his promises to rescue us from the flood and carry us to safety. This waiting can seem endless and needlessly brutal, but in it, the seed of a steadfast heart is taking root.

LORD Jesus, in Psalm 75:3 you assure us that "When the earth and all its people quake, it is I who hold its pillars firm." So we cling to you, we fall at your feet in awe and thank you for who you are, especially when our worlds erupt and fear overwhelms us. Hold us together, Jesus, and save us. Amen.

Have you spoken with God about your fears, and then waited quietly for his response, or been surprised to find it some other way? Give examples.

3
Waiting

I waited patiently for the LORD*;*
he turned to me and heard my cry.
He lifted me out of the slimy pit,
out of the mud and mire; he set my feet on a rock
and gave me a firm place to stand.
Blessed is the one who trusts in the LORD*,*
who does not look to the proud,
to those who turn aside to false gods.
PSALM 40:1-2, 4

"Yes, I'm waiting for answers, for rescue, for comfort—and I'm mad! God, are you punishing us by taking our children? Are you angry and have you abandoned us? You see our anguish, yet you seem to do nothing. Day and night we storm heaven for rescue from this slimy pit, the overwhelming pain of this tragedy. We are suffering! Don't you care? Why don't you stop these evil attacks of the enemy? We wait, we ask 'How long, Lord?' Why don't you hear us?"

As we wait, we're reminded of the mystery that much of life is a battle that God allows, just as he did back in David's time. David frequently complained about God's slowness in responding. But David vowed that he would continue to trust God, no matter how long he had to wait for rescue. We have the same choice, either to trust God or to trust the lies of the world—its false gods, its idolatry. God wants to free us from Satan's lies that lure us to other sources of power and security. He wants to give us David's trust that says, "I believe in you, God, in good times and bad."

Often, what is happening while we wait is a lifting up of our spirit. Holocaust survivor Corrie ten Boom says this[1]: "If you want to hear God's voice clearly and you are uncertain, then remain in His presence until He changes that uncertainty. Often, much can happen during this waiting for

---

[1] Taken from *Not I But Christ* by Corrie ten Boom. Copyright 1984 by Corrie ten Boom. Used by permission of Thomas Nelson. www.thomasnelson.com

the LORD. Sometimes, He changes pride into humility, doubt into faith and peace." God is always working, if we stay in his presence. And where do we find that? The wonder is, we sit right in the midst of his workroom when we spend time in Scripture, absorbing its truths and letting it guide and comfort us. Waiting on God can be restorative. Often, he is rebuilding our hearts and placing us on firmer ground. But this is only the beginning of healing, and there is still hard work ahead with many more emotions to grow through. We try to be patient, but now it seems that the specter of anger is stalking us.

How long, LORD, how long? This tunnel is so
dark and we desperately need your light. We are left
alone, in agony. We need your mercy and your answers.
It's so hard to wait, LORD. We need you. Amen.

Have you realized any changes of heart or mind during your periods of waiting for answers? Are the changes positive or negative?

Anger

You are God my stronghold. Why have you rejected me?
Why must I go about mourning, oppressed by the enemy?
PSALM 43:2

Please don't be ashamed of your anger. We are under vile
oppression by Satan, and we have a right to be angry! He's
convinced us that God no longer cares, and he knows this
thought can cause anger to erupt like a fiery volcano, spewing
everywhere. Get this—anger is the frustrated outpouring of
bottled-up emotion. It indicates the intensity of our love for
our children. The more we truly feel the anger of grief and
release those hurtful emotions, the quicker we'll heal. Most
of us try to suppress anger, but now we find that it has no
limits. It takes over as criticism and sarcasm, withdrawal and
abandonment or crying and screaming. It may be necessary
to go off alone so anger can fully explode. Some of us let loose
by fist-pounding the bed or beating the ground with a stick.
Howling in the car with the windows up also works wonders.
Beneath this anger is pain. We want the clock to turn back
to that hallowed time before. We're angry with people whose
children are still with them. In reality, we're angry with
everyone, even those who are trying to love and help us. It's a
necessary but dangerous time, because anger, if left unexpressed,
can result in bitterness and/or illness.

It may be helpful to realize that anger is often the
first emotion we feel against the nothingness of loss. It often
surfaces once you become aware that you will probably survive
whatever is ahead. In this sense, it's a temporary but valuable
bridge to the real world. Anger may be directed at a person—
for example, someone who didn't attend the funeral or who
said the wrong thing—or at the doctor or family member who
wasn't helpful. We may also experience anger at ourselves or
our child who has left, or at God. You may ask, "Where is God
in this? How could he let this happen?" In the wake of tragedy,

it's natural to feel abandoned by God, and it's okay to be angry with him. He understands and he can take it.

Scripture tells us that death was never part of God's plan. It's not his will for anyone to die. Death is Satan's strategy that God, in his unfathomable wisdom, is allowing for a time. Because he understands our grief, we can trust him to lovingly accept all of our feelings. Ask him anything, even the hard questions. He will respond, although he may be silent for a while, the way a mother quietly holds a child having a tantrum. But he hears and fights for us, so there's no need for vengeful thoughts or prolonged bitterness. God works out the details in his own time, even to the point of giving anger a positive side. Because anger is an excellent teacher, when the emotions subside it may fuel the fight for a good cause (such as MADD or Mothers Against Drunk Drivers). But then, as the smoke clears, we see that our anger has created discomfort for others, and we slide into another difficult stage, that of guilt.

Please bring order and clarity to our tortured minds, Father, and send the still, small voice of the Holy Spirit to propel us toward Jesus. Then, armed not simply with anger but with your power and love, we can meet the challenges of this grief, and find peace with you. Amen.

Think about ways you've found to express your anger over the death of your child. List some here.

Guilt

Listen to my prayer, O God, do not ignore my plea;
hear me and answer me.
My thoughts trouble me and I am distraught
because of what my enemy is saying,
because of the threats of the wicked;
for they bring down suffering on me and assail me in their anger.
PSALM 55:1-3

Hang on, here comes yet another big challenge—because as
we face and deal with anger, we get to meet its unfriendly
partner, guilt. And guilt shoves us even deeper into the depths
of our grief. Troubling thoughts, the "if onlys" and "what ifs,"
take over. Regrets abound, as we long to relive the past while
obsessing over what we could have done differently. As the
psalmist says, we're troubled and distraught. We still cannot
think clearly and as mothers, we're very good at guilt. From the
moment of our baby's conception and for the rest of his or her
life, if something goes wrong, we feel guilty. Our main goal has
been to protect our precious child from hurt, even a skinned
knee or a bump on the head. But there's no way to fix this
hideous, unbelievable thing that has happened. Guilt makes
everything worse. We place blame, sometimes on ourselves,
sometimes on others, and both actions cause harm. Illness
can set in, relationships can be lost and hearts bruised and
broken. The sad part is that many times we are harboring false,
unjustified guilt. When we recognize this, we must reject it as
another assault by that old Enemy, Satan, whose goal is to cause
even more pain.

As with fear, it's good to talk out our guilty feelings. The
real picture often emerges when we share our concerns with
someone we trust. In time we'll see more clearly, and if self-
guilt is justified by things we've said, done, or not done, we
can face those failures with sorrow and regret, and go to Jesus.
There we can pour out our pain and experience his immediate
and complete forgiveness. Also, anyone we have blamed or hurt

deserves an apology and a thank-you for being in our lives. The acts of apologizing, thanking, forgiving and asking forgiveness are big boosts to our healing. This is the blessing of guilt, when we're forced to look at our mistakes—justified or not— and to seek restoration. It's a difficult process, but it's where grace and the Holy Spirit love to show up (as they usually do, when we're attempting something worthwhile). Yes, this road has been rocky and unpredictable. But there's more, with the hardest stretches hidden around the bend. And suddenly, right in the midst of fighting this battle, weakness takes over and proves that we need Jesus more than ever.

Dearest LORD Jesus, please give us your vision as we tackle the threats of Satan's wicked demons. Let us look back only to learn from our failures. Let us be gentle, forgiving ourselves and others while we keep our focus on you and where you're leading us. Amen.

Is there someone whose forgiveness you need to seek, or who deserves thanks for ways they helped that weren't acknowledged? (Don't forget to include Jesus in this review).

6
Weakness

He reached down from on high and took hold of me;
he drew me out of deep waters.
He rescued me from my powerful enemy, from my foes,
who were too strong for me.
They confronted me in the day of my disaster,
but the LORD was my support
(PSALM 18:16-18).

The New Mexico sun beat down on my head as the hearse pulled away from the curb. "Good bye, Baby," I sobbed over and over, as my child's body was slowly carried away, down the hill and out of sight. My knees buckled and I held onto the dear one next to me for support. All I could think was, "The enemy, cancer, won." And now it was mocking me, laughing at my disaster, my loss, my weakness. There's no way in this world to replace the life of a child. Nothing even comes close. We are defeated and broken, and all strength is gone—all energy and optimism and courage. All those qualities that served us so well as mothers departed with our child. We need God's rescue.

Helpless and weak, we are forced to rely on God every minute. And that's when his power takes hold of us, when we say "… only God can help." He truly is our burden-bearer, inviting us to radical dependence on him. I remember a pastor's response when he was accused of using Jesus as a crutch. He answered, "No, not a crutch! He's more like a stretcher that carries me around all day!" Though we may work hard at being strong and independent, we eventually learn that powerlessness is the first step toward healing, freedom and trust in Jesus. So when you're feeling particularly weak, climb onto his stretcher and let him carry you. He reaches down and lifts us up, he loves us and will not leave us helpless. And now more than ever, we need to depend on him, because we're about to sink into the deepest pit of all, the one called "depression."

Please rescue me, Jesus. I'm weak and can't find my way through this disaster without you. I see that weakness is a blessing that has brought me to your feet. I'm not sure if I can get through life without my dear child, _____.
I need you, LORD. I rely on your great power. Please hold me up.

Are you developing the habit of relying on God when you're feeling helpless? How can you turn your weakness over to him and rest in him?

Depression

Then they cried to the LORD in their trouble,
and he saved them from their distress.
He brought them out of darkness, the utter darkness,
and broke away their chains.
PSALM 107:13-14

Watch out! This journey is hard and getting harder. After the downhill plunge into shock, we ricochet off grief's other painful boulders and finally hit rock bottom with depression. It's a dark abyss, with no way to climb out. We claw and scream, but we're trapped in this cave, lost and hopeless. Heavy chains hold us and we can barely move. Life is utterly dark, and our only need is to be with our child. It's a dreadful place.

Grief becomes depression when we lose interest in ourselves and the world and appear to give up the journey. Grief is often seen as an emotional challenge, but depression brings physical problems as well. Much of our being has shut down to protect our spirit, resulting in an array of symptoms. Psalm 102:4 says: "My heart is blighted and withered like grass; I forget to eat my food." The grief experts recommend that we make self-care paramount at this time—eat, sleep and outdoor exercise. How does God respond to depression? In the book of Elijah, he sent an angel with the order to "Get up and eat." Also, remember to breathe and invite the Holy Spirit in with each breath. Ten slow, deep breaths in a row will usually calm us down or help us up. But here's the really big secret for managing depression: at the very top of God's self-care list is prayer and time in the Bible. Here we stay close to him, strengthened by his promises, and that may well be the food he recommended to Elijah.

Just know that this painful stage can last for months, maybe years, and often returns when triggered, as when a birthday or anniversary looms. We are reminded that depression is not a sign of mental illness, but rather the correct response to severe loss. Sometimes we may be advised to "snap out of it"—that depression is unnatural, a state to be avoided at all costs. But those of us who travel this road know better. We know that to experience depression at a time of such severe tragedy is a necessary step to healing, and it's wise to stay with this stage until we've found its blessings.

The most valuable blessing of depression is that in its darkness, we recognize our desperate need for Jesus. When we throw our hurting selves into his arms, and focus on his ability to help us—asking, trusting and staying close to him, we are well on our way out of this deep cave. But as we emerge, many new challenges threaten. One is the dreaded intruder, anxiety.

O God, it seems that only you are with us here, only you know this pain. You created us and our one-of-a-kind child and you planned our lives from the beginning. We want to trust you, but it's so hard to see in the dark, so please bring your light and break these chains. Amen.

Can you trust that Jesus will bring you through this grief? Think about ways he has helped you in the past. Write them here.

8:

Anxiety

Have mercy on me, my God, have mercy on me,
for in you I take refuge.
I will take refuge in the shadow of your wings
until the disaster has passed.
I am in the midst of lions; I am forced to dwell among ravenous
beasts—men whose teeth are spears and arrows, whose tongues are
sharp swords.
PSALM 57:1, 4

Now we must brace ourselves, because we are about to be
attacked by the cruel, ravenous beast, anxiety. With it, a
nearly unbearable burden invades our souls at the slightest
provocation. The psalmist says that we are thrust into the
midst of lions, where we become paralyzed and hopeless. Or
that we need to arm against spears, arrows and sharp swords
flung our way, while at the same time, take refuge from the
new enemies that accompany anxiety—stress and panic attacks.
All this occurs because we're beginning to face the reality of
our situation. Besides the dread of living without our child,
we become anxious that more tragedy may occur and we
wonder how we'll ever survive. It's a time when the numbness
of earlier stages feels like a much kinder place. Because we
have experienced the worst that can happen, anxiety can easily
replace optimism about our future and block efforts to learn
new ways of coping. This failure to cope will cause even greater
anxiety and continue the downward spiral. Airing our worries
with a friend, pastor or therapist can prevent anxiety from
taking over. If we attempt to suppress our feelings in hopes
they'll fade over time, it's like forcing air into a balloon. Soon
the balloon will burst under pressure. This pressure in our
lives can bring about excessive worry and/or panic attacks, and
maybe even an anxiety disorder. At this point, professional help
may be needed, as an important aspect of God's care.

Speaking of anxiety, I read a woman's horrendous story
about her five young children who were murdered by an invader

in her home, while she was out. My mind nearly blew up over
this. How could you ever leave your house again? Wouldn't you
attack anyone who came to your door after that? How would you
ever find the courage to bring more children into such a world?
But this mother, bolstered by God's strength and mercy, was
able to forgive and overcome. She and her husband were blessed
with a second family and an enormous trust in God that defies all
logic. Now she writes to console parents of 9/11 victims.

Anxiety—like depression—is to be expected in the face
of overwhelming loss like ours. And though it's natural to
worry about the future, worry isn't productive. In fact, it's a
failure to trust God, and it will return again and again until
we embrace the reality of our loss, and see clearly all the ways
God is caring for us. The Psalms tell us to pour out our hearts
to him and then hand over our anxious worries. This keeps the
Enemy at bay. So the next time worry sneaks in, turn it into
something useful—let it lead you to God in prayer. Take your
worries to the one in charge!

*Dearest Savior, we believe your wings cover us in
this great disaster, and that with the comfort and guidance
of the Holy Spirit, you are helping us overcome our season
of worry and fear. Thank you, LORD, for your mercy.*

When you recognize that you are obsessively worrying
about your family or your future, do you pour out your
concerns to God? What are other ways that help you refocus?

Prayer

LORD, you are the God who saves me; day and night I cry out to you.
May my prayer come before you; turn your ear to my cry.
PSALM 88:1-2

"Are you there?" I shout. "Can you hear me?" But then, why
would God want to hear my sad story and see my tears again?
Could he possibly love me this much? Does he actually want
to save me, to keep me from falling off a cliff or sinking into
quick-sand? Is prayer really the answer? I ask, because it often
seems futile. Our daughters' lives were not spared, though I
prayed night and day, with tearful pleas. When that prayer
went unanswered, I could have chosen to reject God because
he didn't respond the way I hoped. And that's Satan's goal, to
make us turn away, assuring our destruction. Yes, I was angry,
struck down, shaken. But somehow I knew that giving up on
God would only lead to deeper despair. We read that Abraham
Lincoln once said, "I have been driven many times to my knees
by the overwhelming conviction that I had nowhere else to go."

In our grief, our desperate spirits cry out for connection
with God, because he's the only one who can really help.
Prayer provides that connection, and this may be the first time
we have recognized how much we need it. But prayer can be
terrifying. What might be asked of us now? We are already
astounded at the wretches we've become, the unfamiliar
emotions that plague us. We can barely look in the mirror, let
alone look at God. Facing him is no easy matter, but in our
desperation, we cry out like David in this psalm. And God
turns his ear to us because it's the connection he longs for, to be
with us as Father, Abba, Daddy.

Aren't you grateful for the many ways God can be
reached—especially now, when we can hardly put two words
together? Some days it's just a whispered "thank you" when
we've made it through without falling apart, which is proof
that he is there, carrying us. Or we can simply speak the name

of Jesus, one of the most effective prayers of all. And there's my all-time favorite, the short, urgent "Help!" Even if we can manage only an agonized wail, God hears. In fact, we're assured that the Holy Spirit will complete our prayer for us. "In the same way, the Spirit helps us in our weakness. We do not know what we ought to pray for, but the Spirit himself intercedes for us through wordless groans" (Romans 8:26).

Often, response to prayer appears in Scripture, as a few phrases of assurance like a firm rock to stand on. In them, we know we have a good Father who walks with us every day and listens and waits. Someone said, "When you think to pray, it's because you've heard God calling your name." So throughout the day, let those wisps of longing, remembering, asking and thanking float from your heart to his. He will catch them, listen, and love you through all of this. He will hold you even if your only prayer is a pool of tears.

Father, please teach us to pray well and often as you lead us through this dark valley. Remind us that prayer is the key to our healing, and it brings you glory. Thank you for your Psalms. We know they're perfect models for our prayers because they were prayed and sung by Jesus—so we make them ours.

What are some of your thoughts and feelings after a time of prayer? Do you think of God as a Santa Claus who gives you exactly what you ask for? Or a loving Father who loves you enough to teach you all good things, even the hard stuff? Are you willing to learn?

Tears

Record my misery;
list my tears on your scroll;
are they not in your record?
PSALM 56:8

For Sara

A flood of tears has filled my heart
        since you left to meet the King—
But I saw you last night in a gossamer gown,
        as you flashed that famous grin,
Then you danced a step, saying,
        "Hi! I'm with Jesus! Come along when you can!"
My wee tiny redheaded girl,
        my "hugger" who grew like a willow,
Uniquely your own, wholeheartedly God's,
        you left us his hope and a smile,
And the sun will dry some of our tears,
        and warm our hearts for a while.

There was a time when I laughingly claimed to possess the "gift of tears." At every occasion, both happy and sad, I'd cry openly. Now I view this blessing with awe, realizing that grief has magnified its value a thousand-fold. If your eyes look like mine, they're tired and sad, swollen from sleepless nights and the misery of what they've seen and endured. Perhaps God knows our eyes need soothing and cleansing, so he gives us tears for that purpose.

       Grief comes in waves and its tears can be a hurricane, pounding the floodgates, ready to erupt at a moment's notice. So we weep, often all day—or in brief, inconvenient downpours. Sometimes we have to evacuate, leave this dangerous place to find relief from grief's gale-force winds and rain. But it's not wise to sandbag our emotions for long, as grief needs expression in order to heal, and tears are essential to the process. They self-sooth, release endorphins, ease physical and emotional pain, relieve stress, and aid sleep. But it's good to check with a doctor if crying is overly frequent and uncontrollable, as this can be a sign of clinical depression. Otherwise, it's best to let them flow, because bottled up tears can lead to hardened hearts that are immune to the pain of others and far from Christ. I think of a dear family member who, in her lonely last days, remained stoic and proud of the fact that she never once cried after her husband's death years before. She was stuck, still angry at him, with a joyless bitterness that darkened her life.

Please realize that your poor heart has been cracked wide open. Did you think none of it would ever spill out? Tears are blessings, so when the Holy Spirit prompts you to cry, give in. There is neither shame nor weakness in this, only relief and the tender expression of your love. Letting others see your tears gives them permission for honest sharing of your grief. God's words in this psalm make us realize—with wonder—that he is so intimately involved in our misery that he records every detail, and keeps track of all our tears! As they fall, he saves them in a crystal jar like treasured jewels because they were shed in love and they're beautiful. Better yet, tears are signs of our closeness to Christ in his suffering—and that is the most priceless blessing of all.

O Jesus, only you fully understand our heartbreak and love our tears. You see them as seeds that will grow into a harvest of joy, because you bring good out of tragedy. We believe, Lord, please help our unbelief.

When tears well up, how do you feel? Embarrassed, overly-emotional, or accepting of your pain? How do you respond when a conversation brings you to tears and someone says, "I'm sorry I made you cry"?

11

A Broken Heart

The LORD is close to the brokenhearted
and saves those who are crushed in spirit.
PSALM 34:18

We sometimes think of our tears as warning flares yelling, "Hey, something's broken down there!" It's our heart, the all-important generator that sparks our lives—our physical and mental selves as well as our emotions and spirits. When we speak of a broken heart in grief, we're referring to the emotions that originate in our spirits and affect our bodies. Here we experience pain, loss, sadness and disbelief, and many times this spiritual heart gets battered and broken. But not like this. When her child's earthly life ends, a mother's heartbreak is beyond description.

So it was when Mary stood watching her Son on the cross, her spiritual heart was pierced and shattered. We have to ask, "Why on earth did Jesus allow this to happen to his own mother?" Then we read that from the cross he gave Mary into the safekeeping of his beloved friend, John, as comfort to both of them. And we realize that, as with everything Jesus did, he had a reason. It may have been to show us that, just as he loved and cared for his mother in her brokenness, he does the same for us. He gives us Mary, his grieving mother, to be one with us, and his loving care for her is soothing balm for our own hurting hearts.

When we understand that our spirits—our invisible, non-material parts that hold our unique personalities, memories, desires and dreams—are actually crushed, it's no wonder we don't know ourselves anymore! Can we ever recover? But God... this is where he shines. In *A Spectacle of Glory*, Joni Eareckson Tada[2] writes, "Emotional pain creates an emptiness that refuses to be crowded out of your heart. That's where... God steps in. He holds you in the palm of His hand. He hides

2   Taken from *A Spectacle of Glory* by Joni Eareckson Tada. Copyright 2016 by Joni Eareckson Tada. Used by permission of Zondervan. www.zondervan.com.

you in the cleft of His rock. He shelters you underneath His wings. He is never nearer than when your heart is breaking."

Spiritual heartache and physical heart pain are connected, and even though our physical hearts are not actually broken, they can suffer damage. Recently I read about "broken heart syndrome," a medical condition sometimes caused by grief. When the heart is in constant pain, agitation and stress, the unusual activity can create a weakening of valves and arteries, and throw the heartbeat into irregularity. For me, my broken heart required a pacemaker to help it adjust.

Where is the blessing in this brokenness? One good we can see is that a broken heart opens us to others. We recognize great pain and reach out in love. Though our suffering is far from over, we live in a world where others need compassion, and often we are the only ones who understand. Someone said, "Maybe this is why our hearts break—to make room for more love. Perhaps this is why they mend, too, so that in our healing, we can love again." So here's my heart, Lord. Teach it to love in the midst of suffering. May we become your help and hope for others.

Dear Holy Spirit, please speak healing and strength to our broken hearts as you hold us together now. You, who embody the mind and thoughts of Jesus, help us to see the doors you open. Let us walk through them with soft hearts that spread your love to those you give us.

What would you list as the characteristics of a healed, open spiritual heart?

12

Suffering

My God, my God, why have you forsaken me?
Why are you so far from saving me,
so far from my cries of anguish?
For he has not despised the suffering of the afflicted one;
he has not hidden his face from him
but has listened to his cry for help.
PSALM 22:1, 24

Many times we are confronted by the cross and our hearts break all over again, trying to understand God's will in our suffering. Dear Jesus, you cried the words of this psalm to your Father on that awful day, as your physical suffering was compounded by separation from him. And now in our anguish—our separation from our children—we understand some small fraction of your pain and that of the Father as he watched.

We mothers need no reminders of how our child's earthly life ended. Some of us had time to tend those precious bodies before they left, while others sat with them after the leaving. A few will never see or know, which may carry the greatest anguish of all. These memories are the most painful a mother will ever experience. As time goes on, suffering abates only slightly and as the psalmist says, we often feel forsaken.

So where is the blessing in anguish and suffering? The Bible has much to say on this topic, with phrases like "displaying the work of God," "standing firm," "joy in the midst of," and "being rescued." In a way, these blessings are similar to what heartbreak teaches. It prepares us for what others need, the gift of helps. Listen to this quote by a terminally ill cancer patient: "Life isn't fair and part of the solution is community; you stand shoulder-to-shoulder with others who are suffering." So shoulder-to-shoulder, we really aren't forsaken; rather, we realize that in his sovereign will, God chose this way to make us holy, while standing with us in our suffering. And now, life becomes a giant relay race, as what we receive from him—the "standing with"—we then pass off to another. We are sensitive to others' needs and we know how to help. And when they see us remaining faithful to God in our pain, they are affected for good. The race gets even better when, as we help others, they see Jesus—his compassion, mercy and love. Finally, the relay comes full circle because in the simple kindnesses we offer, Jesus is glorified, and in this, our suffering abates. Even so, we must continue to look to him for hope, because soon sorrow will be moving in for the long haul.

O Jesus, thank you for the privilege of experiencing your suffering. It isn't easy for us to consider suffering a privilege (and we would never have chosen this way), so we ask for the will to submit to your plan. As we grow closer to you, please open our hearts to others. In this way, may our suffering bring you honor.

Sit quietly and ask the Holy Spirit for encouragement in your suffering. Listen until words form. Write them here and memorize them, repeating them over and over. This is your blessing today. Praise him for it.

Sorrow

My *soul is weary with sorrow;*
strengthen me according to your word.
PSALM 119:28

Yes, our souls are weary because, like its cousin depression,
sorrow seems to stay forever, and we become very tired of
living in its darkness. Though we function more normally
than we did with depression, heavy clouds still block the sun
and suffocate our hearts with dread and gloom. Sorrow spreads
deep into our souls—our essential, eternal selves—and colors
all our days with longing. It is probably the most universally-
experienced symptom of grief, and the most effective weapon of
the Enemy. In his aim to destroy us, he seems to triumph. This
is because there's no time limit to sorrow. It can't be rushed,
so we need to overlook the advice of those who say it's time to
"move on." Just know that our hearts will ache with sorrow for
much longer than we expect.

Sorrow soup is served with each meal,
  A miserable mix of memories and loss,
A dish of the Enemy and his hateful plan
  To destroy what Jesus has done for us.
But God... O God, you have won.
  For us.

  The Holy Spirit reminds us of the futility of hiding our
feelings on those dark days. He inspires us instead, to journal
our thoughts and worries or talk them over with a friend. Or
find his comfort in Scripture. It seems our life is over, but in
reality, we're getting a new one—one that mirrors the truth
and strength of his Word. Like a dim light in the distance, the
awareness of living in God's presence begins to emerge. And
in that presence the darkness cannot stand. That's because
when we look to our Savior as our source of strength and
redemption, he brings us back to himself and we see him in a

bright new way. He has defeated the Enemy and our sorrow is being transformed into newness and purpose. This is his perfect blessing to us. For us.

O Lord, I'm so tired of this sorrow. Please hold me as I grieve for _____, *the beautiful child I miss so much. Carry me until I'm stronger, Jesus, especially in my loneliness, and I will know you and believe.*

"With God we will gain the victory, and he will trample down our enemies" (Psalm 108:13). Think about what this verse means to you. You might want to memorize and repeat it often. This is God's blessing, to give you hope as you mourn.

Loneliness

I am like a desert owl, like an owl among the ruins.
I lie awake; I have become like a bird alone on a roof.
PSALM 102:6-7

The loneliness of "child-grief" defies description. A mother will never be more alone than she is now, without her child. Her life is an empty ruin—a cold, joyless place where no one waits to be held, loved or cared for. Gone is that dear familiar face, the sweet voice so well-loved, the happy laughter. The bereft mother sits alone and hidden, unwilling to be seen, while grief pushes in on all sides.

Yes, our deepest loneliness is for our children. Nothing can fill that void, and grief has changed us. But though we feel like birds alone on a roof, we still need human warmth and connection—maybe more than ever. Loneliness is a blessing that speaks of our need for others, loud and clear. But often the outside world is aloof, seeming to exclude or avoid us, as if what we have is "catching." Friends are uncomfortable, unsure of what to say, or fearful of causing us unnecessary pain. In *A Grief Observed*, C. S. Lewis offers this poignant thought:[3] "I'm aware of being an embarrassment to everyone I meet... perhaps the bereaved ought to be isolated in special settlements like lepers."

At times, solitude is comforting, but we're told that suffering silently is neither Godly nor particularly healthy. So we welcome those who reach out to us, though there's often the problem of their inability to understand our feelings. But if they acknowledge our grief and let us talk about it, we realize we can live with our pain and also have a normal life, which helps us heal. And often, in a grief support group, Bible study or our church family, the Holy Spirit may put the perfect friend in our path, one we can love like a sister.

Finally, if we listen, we'll hear the Holy Spirit reminding us to spend more time with Jesus in his Word, because he longs

3   Taken from *A Grief Observed* by C. S. Lewis. Copyright 1961 by C. S. Lewis. Used by permission of Thomas Nelson. www.thomasnelson.com.

to enter and fill our hearts. Thus, loneliness becomes blessing when it directs us to the loving arms of Jesus, where we find the most trusted Friend of all, and receive an extra abundance of his love.

He weeps with me under the tamarisk tree...
his tears fall with mine in this wilderness place,

He guards me with care and keeps me safe...
he speaks words I need, of peace, oh peace,

He holds my hand and he binds my weak knees...
to keep me upright so I won't fall far.

My best Friend knows and loves me still...
'til songs of hope fill the air and my heart.

Do you believe that Jesus suffered loneliness and therefore understands ours? When was he most lonely? How did he react when others left him? Where did he turn for comfort and encouragement?

Sleeplessness

I am worn out from my groaning.
All night long I flood my bed with weeping
and drench my couch with tears.
My eyes grow weak with sorrow;
they fail because of all my foes.
PSALM 6:6-7

Night becomes our enemy, because that's when grief really takes over. We toss and turn but in the early weeks, sleep is like quicksilver—impossible to grasp—and we are left worn out and weak. However, for those of us with busy lives and many distractions, night is perhaps the best time for a good cry. So like the psalmist, we might flood our bed with weeping.

Dreams are another reason to dread nighttime. When we do sleep, we often wake in tears, wrenched from dreams of our child's presence. Our arms ache, our hearts lay cracked and bleeding. All our sad thoughts, our foes, rush in to torment us. And we weep, remembering. But dreams can be a mixed bag, even sometimes a blessing. Waking and feeling our child with us can cause a rush of pain combined with happiness. Maybe God knows we need these little gifts to hold at night, these reassurances that he is there, and he cares.

Sleeplessness can also be the opportunity Jesus needs to speak with us. Away from the world and alone with him, our quieted minds may now recall his words of love from Scripture, or times of his past comfort and encouragement. What a sweet interaction, as we hear and respond. Or, if we sleep alone, this can be a time for singing to our LORD, as Paul and Silas did in the jail cell at midnight. We may be blessed with a similar miracle as theirs, where God loosens the chains of sleeplessness and enfolds us in his rest.

During the day we may hear a small alarm clock chiming "It's time." That's the Holy Spirit, urging us to rest. When I hit a brick wall and can't go on, I listen and take a nap. My heart aches for you grieving moms whose responsibilities prevent this luxury. Please find ways to be gentle with yourself. Your suffering is immense, so allow time to do nothing—relax, take in the beauty of nature, find small pleasures. Let healing begin. Psalm 4:8 says "In peace I will lie down and sleep, for you alone, LORD, make me dwell in safety." We abide, resting and moving in and with him, and slowly, slowly we begin to feel safe again. Sleep becomes peaceful—welcome rest for our bodies, minds and hearts. And we find ourselves standing on firmer ground.

We thank you, Jesus, for showing us how you took time away from the crowds to rest, how you took naps in the back of the boat, even during a storm. Help us, in this storm, to care for ourselves in this good simple way.

Do you recognize the Holy Spirit in the simple blessings of your life? Write him a thank-you note here.

16

Safety

*Whoever dwells in the shelter of the Most High
will rest in the shadow of the Almighty.
For he will command his angels concerning you
to guard you in all your ways;
they will lift you up in their hands,
so that you will not strike your foot against a stone.
You will tread on the lion and the cobra;
you will trample the great lion and the serpent.*
PSALM 91:1, 11-13

Today we listen to this promise and hold it to our hearts! In God's shelter and shadow we'll find rest, and soon, safety will also move in! Looking back over our lives, we see clearly that the LORD has kept us safe from many of Satan's plans to hurt us. He surely sent protecting angels that evening when Robin called from her room, asking, "Mom, do you want to see my mastectomy scar?" I froze inside for I had been dreading this moment. Her recent surgery at age thirty had gripped us all with pain beyond words. My eyes filled with tears as she unbuttoned her pajama top. Then, as I gazed at the sweetest image, I knew that my prayers about this moment were heard. There was Robin's "little girl" chest, flat and innocent, with a thin pink scar running across. It was beautiful, and I smiled at her. God gave me that blessing, to be able to smile for this frightened child of mine while he shielded both our hearts, which would be so badly broken later.

I'm sure we all can look back on moments that held the threat of devastation, but which miraculously became a sweet blessing. That's Jesus, sending angels to keep us safe. Recognize that in these small miracles, he's creating us anew, reshaped and made strong in his immovable peace and love. We can endure, we will survive. Yes, with Jesus, we are safe.

But I know we sometimes may think we're losing our minds. Our minds can't be lost, but if we let them, they can take us into unsafe places like despair, substance abuse or denial. Knowing that Satan can entice us when we let down our guard, we constantly depend on the power of Christ to protect us. He is our strongest defense and most trust-worthy guide, our healing ally. Say the name of Jesus when Satan comes near—resist and he will flee. Each day ask for protection because we are traveling through a very dangerous country.

Yes, we have tread on the cobra. We have released our precious children into God's hands. Satan planned this to destroy us, but God has been our guard. We can thank him when we arrive at a place that is safe, even if it isn't quite where we thought we were heading. Jesus will keep us safe and he has a plan. We can rest in his shadow and we can even be open to his light.

Jesus, you are our best Friend; thank you for keeping us safe. Together we say, "Send me your light and your faithful care, let them lead me; let them bring me to your holy mountain, to the place where you dwell" (Psalm 43:3).

Who or what in your life is helping you feel safe right now? Write a prayer thanking God for the ways he is caring for you.

*O*penness

I am feeble and utterly crushed;
I groan in anguish of heart.
All my longings lie open before you, LORD;
my sighing is not hidden from you.
PSALM 38:8-9

OK, everybody, let's "share" our stories! If that thought makes
you cringe, you're not alone. But here our wise God reminds us
of the need to open up our longings and misery to him. Much
healing can be missed when we hide our pain from the light of
God's Word and his boundless love. One way to open up is in
our daily readings, where we may come across a line or phrase
that echoes our concerns that day. Whether it's anger, loneliness,
depression or any number of emotions, repeat the verse he has
given you. Hold it in your heart and elaborate on your pain for
as long as you can, as if he's sitting there with you. Using his
words, ask for help. Then wait quietly for what comes. It may
be a promise, or the warmth of peace, or a special word for you
to keep. But be assured, he will honor your openness with a
blessing, and the safety you're beginning to experience will grow.

Many of us are blessed with friends who actively listen.
For some of us it's a husband or other family member who
can comfort us with shared tears and mutual memories. But
often we feel it's useless to talk about our grief because no
one understands. We may say, "I can handle this alone—this
is too personal to share. If I don't talk about my pain, it'll go
away. Sharing makes it worse." Also, well-meaning friends
or relatives may discourage us from talking about what has
happened because it makes us (or them) feel sad. The truth is,
telling our story is necessary for healing because it reinforces
that our loss mattered.

Hidden emotions can become hauntings which Satan
can use to injure us even more, but we sometimes need help
to feel. We heard a particularly sad story in our grief group

from a dear woman whose son had chosen to end his life. Her devastated husband pulled his grief inside and refused to talk or listen, or even mention their son's name. Thankfully, she found a counselor who helped her open up and examine her story, but her husband's grief was too overwhelming. Pray that he calls out to Jesus for rescue. Reluctance or inability to expose our hearts is a difficult issue in grief, and often words can't express the pain. But be assured, God knows. Trust him and he will send comfort.

Dear Jesus, please sit with me while I search for words—for openness, a way to tell my story. You say, "The journey is too hard for you—you are only dust," so I know you understand. As I lean on you, the way opens.

Does your grief involve hindrances that make it difficult for you to be open? Are there other ways you can tell your story? Do you fear that sharing your story will increase your pain? Why or why not?

Comfort

Even though I walk through the darkest valley,
I will fear no evil, for you are with me;
your rod and your staff, they comfort me.
PSALM 23:4

This I know: one thing we really need on this journey through
the darkest valley is comfort. We've been badly wounded and
we're frightened. Our lives have been wrecked by evil, and
we cringe in desperation. Often we are tempted to look to
the world for comfort. It offers a vast array of possibilities,
but none work and most are destructive. Only God can keep
us comfortable as we make our way. These words, "for you
are with me" are all we need. Visualize walking on this dark
path, guided and comforted by Jesus at your side. With his
rod he protects his sheep, and with his staff he leads them to
safety. We are encouraged by this comfort, which he often
sends by way of others, who arrive with casseroles, tears, hugs
and loving words. Like comfort food, God's presence can warm
and sooth our frozen hearts—and then we get to pass it around
the table, because he now asks us to comfort others as we have
been comforted. Isn't this request one of God's most beautiful
blessings of grief to us? He can use us so well for this work
because he has taught us well.

As grieving mothers, we are grateful for the LORD's
presence and provision, but we also long for the comfort of
knowing where our children are. This is still a mystery to us.
We do know they have not become angels, as some greeting
cards infer. Angels are heavenly beings who serve as God's
messengers. Our children's souls have left their hurt bodies,
and we pray they're with Jesus, but we have no proof. However,
we can make a choice. Even if we aren't absolutely certain that
our child has been saved, we can choose to believe. So I choose
to believe without doubt that my girls woke up to a bright
new morning with Jesus. He promised his disciples and us:

"I will come back and take you to be with me, that you also may be where I am" (John 14:3). When our children's souls left this world, their spirits remained with us, in our love, our remembering, our dreaming and our stories.

Dear Holy Spirit, you are the "Great Comforter," and though we are broken and lost, we know you are holding us with the comfort of a loving parent. Teach us to look to you alone, but please show us the needs of others. Fill us with your compassion— the words and kindnesses that bring you to their wounded lives.

In your grief, where do you find comfort? Do some sources help you more than others? How would you rate each comforting experience in terms of health? (For instance, one of my negative comforts is too much sugar intake.)

19

Compassion

*The LORD upholds all who fall and
lifts up all who are bowed down.*
PSALM 145:14

"Jesus wept." His friends were suffering and in his compassion, he found ways to lift them up, to be with them. He said, "Take up your mat and walk," or "Little girl, get up," or "Go and sin no more." He gave us those examples, and because of the comfort we've received, we have eyes to see others with his compassion. Has someone held you while you cried, listened to your fears and sorrow, brought you a lovely flower, taken you to dinner, sent a letter with memories of your child, called you to see how you're doing, prayed with you for healing, spoken your child's name, remembered birthdays and anniversaries or held your hand? That person is a wounded healer, inspired by the Holy Spirit to let the compassion of Jesus flow through them to you. That's Jesus, loving us back to sanity. And he says, "Go and do likewise."

Many of my best memories of growing up in my home town revolved around a small, grey-haired woman we called "Mother" Phillips. Though she had no family, she never seemed lonely. Instead, she devoted her time and energy to making life better for us kids. She organized a youth center in the old school so we could meet and play games, dance and socialize. She gave us art classes too, but best of all, during the summer she arranged for a school bus to take us to the lake for swimming lessons. She made sure we all knew how to swim. I often wondered why we called her "Mother" and why she loved us so much. Later I learned that, years before, her two children had drowned in a boating accident on that lake. She must have been well-comforted in her grief, to have had such great compassion for us.

There are a world of needs and many opportunities for compassion. It may simply involve encouraging someone with a smile or a hug. In fact, hugging may be the most compassionate blessing of all. I'll bet Jesus gave amazing hugs—and lots of them. Let's stay close and keep each other warm in this difficult time. If our broken hearts have begun to heal, they need a little exercise. They need to open, stretch, soften and bless others. Jesus said to go wash someone's feet. It's for our own good, and we don't have to look far. We may have family members who are bowed down and most in need of our loving attention right now.

LORD Jesus, thank you for the stories of compassion we find in your Word. They inspire us to bless those around us with your love, which we know is part of your plan. Use us, Dear Savior— transform our grief into something of value, all for your glory. Amen.

Who can you bless with the compassion of Christ? Ask the Holy Spirit to show you—and then make a list.

20

Family

For the sake of my family and friends,
I will say, "Peace be within you."
PSALM 122:8

In *The Worst Loss*, Barbara Rosof writes this about family:[4]
"When a child dies, parents and siblings are stricken at once
with the same grief. Although the fantasy is that they will
cling to each other and comfort each other, what happens
is often sadly different. Mother sees herself alone on a tiny
life raft. Her husband and children are each on their own
rafts, battered by the same storm. But she is so close to
sinking herself that she must focus all her energy on staying
afloat. Thus, children suffer a second loss—their sibling and
connection with their parents."

A friend whose three children died of a congenital
disease interviewed her surviving children in their adult
years, and here's what they said: "The burden of being a
survivor has been heavy on me. It resulted in overwhelming
sadness, guilt, anger often turned inward, and unresolved
grief." Another spoke of needing his parents' approval as
the one lucky to live. "I felt neglected, alone, left out, not
cherished, without direction, and I questioned God and
his goodness." They agreed that counseling helps, but
not as much as closeness with a parent: holding, talking,
comforting, laughing, reading, walking—any type of
normalcy, whatever their ages. Fathers also need closeness
and compassion—a large order for a bereft mother, who often
depends on him for stability.

In this critical time for the whole family, much of the
future is determined. We are bound together, affecting and
rubbing off on each other. This can be a kind or a hurtful
rubbing. It can heal or wound. Relationships, already made
fragile by stress, can shatter forever—or be stronger, with God.

4   Taken from *The Worst Loss* by Barbara D. Rosof. Copyright 1994 by Barbara D.
Rosoff. Used by permission of Henry Holt.

Yes, all things are possible, even our shaky attempts to console one another at such a time.

My favorite phrase "… but God" now has a partner, "… only God." I use this when an event takes a surprising turn that only he could have orchestrated. I have a snapshot that Lisa, our oldest daughter, caught as I kissed Sara one last time in the hospital. Later, while thanking Lisa for it, I explained that for me it was a holy moment, as if I was releasing Sara into the arms of Jesus. Wide-eyed, Lisa exclaimed, "Mom, I never thought you'd say that!" Neither did I. It was definitely an "… only God" experience, bringing his peace to both of us, and softening Lisa's concern for me. And isn't that how he often works, that when we try to help others sort through feelings and questions, he helps us with our own? That's a remarkable blessing.

Dear LORD, as mothers struggling under heavy burdens, we need your guidance in caring for our families at this time. Help us to see our wounds as "sacred," a way to you, so that we don't transmit our own pain to the rest of our family. Help us to ease their loss and show them your love, for their sake. Amen.

Who needs your compassion now? Have you assumed that other family members are dealing well with this grief? List each one—your child's father, children, siblings, grandparents—maybe a close friend or teacher, anyone who might appreciate time with you to share their memories and feelings. Make a list, make a plan, ask God for guidance.

21

Friends

Restore us, O God; make your face shine on us,
that we may be saved.
PSALM 80:3

Thank God for friends! He uses them to restore us and to shine his face on us in our grief. They are like spark plugs sent just in time, to keep us recharged. Some listen to our pain over and over. They've heard parts of our children's stories many times, and not objected. Some weep with us. Without those who have steadfastly loved and cared for us, I don't know where we'd be right now. Theologian Henri Nouwen wrote this:[5] "When we honestly ask ourselves which persons in our lives mean the most to us, we often find that it is those who, instead of giving advice, solutions, or cures, have chosen rather to share our pain and touch our wounds with a warm and tender hand. The friend who can be silent with us in a moment of despair or confusion, who can stay with us in an hour of grief and bereavement, who can tolerate not knowing, not curing, not healing and face with us the reality of our powerlessness, that is a friend who cares."

God has been present to me in many precious friends. Some I've known for years and others I met at grief group and Bible study tables. These friends have truly blessed me with God's heart—with his compassion, encouragement and wisdom. They have helped restore me with a new identity as one who is learning to genuinely trust God. They have shown me that we are all connected and that God takes part in our suffering. Strongest and most loving among them has been my husband Patrick, my best friend. He has taught me that we must learn to be shared, to sit at the group table instead of alone and apart. It's good to stay connected. There may be others who need to hear our story, for only God knows what their futures may hold, and our influence may be the very thing he can use to save them.

---

5   Taken from *Out of Solitude* by Henri Nouwen. Copyright 1974 by Henri Nouwen. Used by permission of Ave Maria Press.

One Bible study friend who I met during my early days of grief was Melanie. She was young and she came to us with such grace, asking for prayers to heal her cancer. We all loved her dearly, and were broken-hearted when we heard that she had gone Home to God. He gave me these words for her mother, Cindy.

Melanie

She drifted into our midst, soft as gentle morning dew,
And we were drawn to her as to a delicate thing,
    Like a fawn or a bird or a beautiful bloom.
As she told her story, we were stunned and surprised,
    And we reached out in loving hope.
Now we bless you, her mother, and share your pain,
    In the sweetness that flows from your heart to ours.

Thank you, Jesus, for shining your face on us through your blessing of friends. We are assured that "Though you have made me see troubles, many and bitter, you will restore my life again" (Psalm 71:20). Let us befriend others who need to sit at the group table, so they may see your face and find restoration.

Take time to write or call friends who have walked with you through your grief. Tell them specifically how they have helped you. Pray for them, that God will tenderly bless their life.

22

*P*eace

Then they cried out to the LORD in their trouble,
and he brought them out of their distress.
He stilled the storm to a whisper;
the waves of the sea were hushed.
PSALM 107:28-29

I'm wondering if you related, as I did, to the image in the devotional on Family? "Mom sees herself alone, on a tiny life raft." As we grieve for our children, haven't we felt like that—storm-tossed and barely hanging on? Yet we are assured in this psalm that the LORD will bring us out of our distress and still the storm to a whisper. He asks only that we cry out to him, and he will carry us to a peaceful place—a place of fair winds and calm seas. Then we can repeat the words of Horatio Spafford's hymn, *It Is Well With My Soul.* Spafford (1828-1888) had a prosperous life until tragedy took his five children and most of his wealth. He turned to God and was inspired to write this song of serenity, which begins: "When peace like a river, attendeth my way, when sorrows like sea billows roll; Whatever my lot, Thou hast taught me to say, 'It is well, it is well, with my soul.'"

How comforting to know that in the midst of this great pain, God can give us peace, peace like a river. He leads us out of a dark, terrifying woods onto a riverbank of calm. Easing in, we let the water gently carry us along on this journey. With such peace, we can say, "Whatever my lot, Thou hast taught me to say, it is well ...." We feel no fear or dread because Jesus is both our guide and friend, and we have found this peace in his presence. To desire deeper relationship with him, to be willing to listen and trust—that is the key. It's a tall order in this terrible tragedy, but it's possible and necessary for our healing. At the feet of Jesus, we discover how to accept and trust his timing and perfect will, in what he has allowed in our lives. This is where we find peace of mind that will bring us through the storm.

The best way to know and trust Jesus is to love Scripture—because that's where he is, in his Word. There, in stories and promises and praise, God's heart opens and we find our own revived. Each morning while I read my Bible, my little cat jumps into my lap. She seems to know this is a time of peace and healing, so she curls her softness into me, with loud purring and happy "kneading." Thank you for her love, LORD. Thank you for your simple moments of peace. Thank you for the blessing of knowing you in your Word.

Merciful LORD Jesus, please guide us out of the storm. In this great struggle, only your peace can save us. Only you can calm this anxiety, depression, weakness and heartbreak with a whisper. In this peaceful place, our hearts can be restored and our souls can be healed. Thank you, Jesus.

Where or how do you find peace? What peace is the Holy Spirit placing in your heart right now?

23
The Word

Remember your word to your servant, for you have given me hope.
My comfort in my suffering is this:
Your promise preserves my life.
I remember, LORD, your ancient laws,
and I find comfort in them.
PSALM 119:49, 50, 52

What is this book, this ancient tome?
      Who penned these words so true?
Who knew creation at its birth? Whose love warms every page?
      And why? To touch my wretched heart—
      or my mind which asks "O why?"
Or my soul that cries throughout the night,
      a prisoner chained and cold?
It's a book of comfort and peace and hope,
      with gifts to heal our days,
And songs that tell the blessed news,
      for those who weep and pray.
We hear our Father speak to us with promises we can hold,
As Love, uncommonly strong and true,
      Holds our grief as his own.

And there's light for the uncertain path ahead,
      the road that leads to Home,
With guidance and goodness to keep us safe,
      blessed forevermore.
There's abundance of help to grow our faith
      and show us how to live,
In parables, poems, hosannas and praise,

      and the angels sing for joy.

It's Jesus the Word, God-sent to earth!
  Our Savior, our King, our Way.
He tells us he loves us, he touches our pain
  in mercy and healing grace.
He's here in this book, holy and real,
  precious as gold and myrrh.
Come see, O come see and taste what is good!
  He waits, he calls, he is here.

Careful, watch your step! The path is rocky and we can easily stumble in the dark! But look, there's a light shining, just enough to save us. "Your word is a lamp for my feet, a light on my path" (Psalm 119:105). Words from the Bible, inspired by the Holy Spirit, can guide us through any of Satan's snares and point the way to God's Kingdom. The Bible is not only our light but also our daily bread and the main means of healing our grief. It's nourishment that ensures health and growth for our spirit. Even a small amount of the Word each day, taken with prayer and thought and desire, gives us Jesus. As we take him in, we see that, in our grief, he is teaching us mysteries we could never otherwise know. His blessings are as surprising and perfect as what we find, gazing into the tide pools at Half Moon Bay. Look and be amazed by God's Word. In it, there's hope for our hearts, with assurance and reassurance.

Thank you, Jesus, for the inestimable blessing of knowing you in the Bible. Especially now, in our grief, we find healing for our sick souls and all the comfort, nourishment and guidance of a good parent. Your Word is your love letter to us, promising your help in this struggle. And we say "Amen."

Have you memorized any part of the Bible? How have those verses helped you in your grief?

24

Assurance

My frame was not hidden from you
when I was made in the secret place,
when I was woven together in the depths of the earth.
Your eyes saw my unformed body;
all the days ordained for me were written in your book
before one of them came to be.
PSALM 139:15-16

Go back! Imagine those days before you came to be—before
your body was formed in the "secret place." God saw you then,
he knew you through and through. In fact, he had already
written your life story in his book. And he loved you so much—
he always has and always will. These verses are especially for us
and our children, and what comfort they are!

The whole Bible is one big assurance that God knows us
completely—spirit, soul, mind and body. His thoughts of us
are as numerous as the grains of sand on the seashore because he
is our parent and we are his well-loved children. "I am with you
always," he promises. May his Word penetrate our hearts so we
can believe. We can know for sure that in a world of continuous
change—where nothing lasts—God is always the same. As our
Father, he knows all the details of our lives—even when we feel
like we're living in the Land of the "Uns." We feel unbalanced,
unable, unsure, unknowing, unbelieving and unhappy. He
knows, and he promises to deliver us and light our way. Before
the beginning of time, he planned the length and purpose of
our lives. Best of all, because of the cross, when the Father looks
at us, he sees Jesus. This is blessed assurance that we are his
children and his great love for us will never waver.

But one big question arises. It's the one that asks, "If
God's love for us is so great, why didn't he protect our children?
Why did their lives end so soon?" We try to trust, but we
wonder why a loving God allowed this to happen. His Word
assures us that all his ways are good, and that in his ability and
power, we can do all he's called us to do. But we have doubts,

so we pray for patience and perseverance to find the answer, so we can be reassured and say, "Whatever my lot, LORD ...."

I can't fix this, but God can.
       When tears come, God holds me.
I don't know how this will end,
       but God knows.
I see no sense in this,
       but God does.
When it's hard to accept,
       God understands.
His ways are not our ways,
       but they are always perfect.
Thank you, Jesus, for taking

_____ Home with you
       at just the right time.

Bless you, Dear Savior, for knowing how much we need you, and for loving us unconditionally. You give yourself to us through your Word and through others. May we open our lives to your tender, elusive butterfly of assurance, and let it light in our minds, hearts and spirits as a quiet, abiding symbol of your love.

What assurances are you finding as you grieve for your child? It might help, as you study the Bible, to write the verses that offer assurance about God's goodness. Verses like, "... for God so loved the world that he gave..." (John 3:16).

25

Protection

The LORD is gracious and righteous;
our God is full of compassion.
The LORD protects the unwary;
when I was brought low, he saved me.
PSALM 116: 5-6

O LORD, we are assured of your love, but still we cry out for answers. Why weren't our children protected? Why didn't you save us from this dreadful grief? Your psalms tell us that you hear our cry and see our pain. But oh, how hard it is to accept that you chose us mothers to endure this, not as punishment but as a blessing. Most difficult of all is to see your plan as good—the plan that you would allow our children an early departure from this earth and deprive us of their presence.

This is the story of God's plan and protection for our youngest daughter, Sara. One cold day in early spring, our three little girls were drawn to the forbidden ditch bank, ignoring our strict warnings. Springtime in New Mexico means the irrigation ditches run deep and strong. As our girls stood gaping at the rushing water, the family dog bumped Sara and she tumbled in and sank. God was there and he helped the older sisters rescue her. It had to be God—there was no other way. He said, "No, not yet... Sara has lots more to do. Someday her sister will lead her to me, and she will bring her husband and children along. And one evening a young man will come to sit with her mother in the hospice unit. He will tell, with grateful tears, how his faith in me was sparked when Sara simply held out her hand to him and smiled 'Shalom.' That one word led to his salvation."

Then God said to Sara, "Now it's time, your work is complete. Come Home to me, to your glory." That night Sara's husband read Psalm 23 to her, and he came to verse 6: "Surely your goodness and love will follow me all the days of my life, and I will dwell in the house of the LORD forever."

At that, Sara opened her eyes, looked up, and slipped into
waiting arms. Two years later, her sister followed her. This
was his perfect plan.

But we often need help to fathom the unfathomable
and see God's compassion in his plan. Most importantly, we
need to realize that when we are brought low, God protects us
in our pain, not *from* it. We need to see that when we call, he
lifts us up and gives us his Word—with its shields of truth,
peace, wisdom, faith and courage to protect us in the battles of
life. Most of all, we need assurance that when we give our lives
to Jesus—accept his salvation—he will not allow the Enemy
to win. We will know that this life is not all there is, and that
suffering is allowed because it draws us most closely to him.
Satan may end our earthly lives, but it is Jesus who saves our
souls and takes us to live in his heavenly realm forever.

*Jesus, our Messiah, please help us to trust this plan
of yours and to be still and quiet, willing to learn what
you have to teach us in this grief. Thank you that our
children are now with you, bright shining as the sun.*

How have you experienced God's protection in the past?
Write your story here:

26

Quiet

He says, "Be still, and know that I am God;
I will be exalted among the nations,
I will be exalted in the earth."
PSALM 46:10

Often my mouth is my worst enemy. Though we Irish may call it "the gift of gab," the Bible tells us to "be still," a request my husband might sometimes make, as my teachers did years ago. A plaque in our home proclaims this verse as a gentle reminder. I am acutely aware of my tendency to speak in every situation, and not always with the greatest tact. In a recent Bible study, we were discussing God's glory—his splendor, majesty, beauty and honor—and the question was thrown out, "Where would you like to see God's glory in your life?"

"In my mouth!" I responded when my turn came. Everyone laughed, but I was quite serious. I was including quality along with quantity, wishing to choose my words with more care and keep them kind—devoid of anger, sarcasm or other hurtful tones—and to think and pray before speaking. In grief, some of us do tend to talk a lot while others clam up, and neither extreme is helpful. In the devotion on Openness, we explored the importance of telling our story as a necessary step to healing. But over-focusing on the details of our grief, with endless discussing and complaining, can make grief our tightly-gripped "identity," and block God's work of transformation in us.

Psalm 46 urges us to "be still," along with the words "and know." Only in stillness, quiet and being alone, can we truly begin to "know" our God and what he has done and is doing in our lives. We need quiet moments to hear the still, small voice of the Holy Spirit, whispering that God is fully in charge, he has perfect plans for our lives, he loves us deeply and we can trust him. None of what happens is a surprise to God, and we will benefit most if we place ourselves in his hands and embrace what he has allowed. He tells us, "Find your peace by being alone with me each day. Choose a quiet place, take on the blessing of stillness and serenity, close your eyes and open your heart."

Dear Holy Spirit, clothe us in stillness so we can dwell on your words and take in your beauty. Help us to imagine Jesus with our children who are now happy, well and blessed. Let us sail with them out over ocean waves to a new land. Show us amazing colors and sights! Let us laugh with abandon, sing with joy!

If a quiet time is not already a part of your daily routine, where and when can you plan for one?

27

Laughter

Our mouths were filled with laughter,
our tongues with songs of joy.
Then it was said among the nations,
"The LORD has done great things for them."
PSALM 126:2

Do you agree that right now, the possibility of tossing your head back in joyful laughter is about as remote as landing on the far side of the moon? Yet studies on the benefits of laughing urge us to find humor in our lives as an aid to healing. At Cedar Sinai Hospital in Los Angeles, the library shelves in the Cancer Unit are stacked with funny videos. While I was there with Robin after her first surgery, we spent entire days in hilarity, inhaling Peter Sellers movies. Our faces hurt, but it was time well spent for both of us.

This psalm makes an even more valuable point in that when we laugh, others see visible proof of the healing work of God in our lives, thus giving him glory. Healing and giving God glory are two great reasons for levity. If we can laugh while we grieve, there's no doubt about the great things he's doing for us. For one, when thoughts of our children make us smile, they seem closer. Enjoying and sharing our funny memories can lighten spirits, lift souls and minds and increase love in our hearts. One of the best memories I have is laughing with Sara during her last days with us. I told her that I wanted to "go Home" with her. Through the morphine haze, she managed a joke. "OK," she said, "let's do it like Thelma and Louise. Go get the car!" I love to share that story with others and see them smile.

Have you made the wonderful discovery that a trip through a photo album can generate enough laughter to fortify the entire family? And of the importance of time with those whacky friends who have fun-loving personalities? Giggling with a girlfriend over lunch is one of the best antidotes to sorrow.

Enjoy other opportunities for laughter, including humorous books and comedy TV shows and movies. You might try my family's regular diet of *America's Funniest Home Videos*, which releases most of the endorphins we need to keep our balance.

Do find ways to have fun. Know that the blessing of laughter improves our countenance and helps us and others to relax. It's one of the LORD's best medicines for these sad times, proving that we have him with and in us, and that he is healing us. We may not be ready to sing songs of joy quite yet, but laughter may place that possibility on our horizon.

Dearest LORD Jesus, thank you for reminding us that the simple blessing of laughter can ease our hearts and lift our spirits. Help us to recognize your promptings when humor, a funny situation or a sweet memory arises, and to see it as your hope, held out to us like a bright light.

For the next few days, try to smile at everyone you meet, both friends and strangers. Take note of how that act affects your mood. What surprises occurred as a result of your smile or laughter?

28

Singing

Praise be to the LORD,
for he has heard my cry for mercy.
The LORD is my strength and my shield;
my heart trusts in him, and he helps me.
My heart leaps for joy,
and with my song I praise him.
PSALM 28:6-7

Yes, here's another big challenge. And yes, the LORD has been our strength and he deserves our praise. But for us who grieve, singing is the last thing we feel like doing! Knowing this brings us to another of my "fall back on" comments—"so God ...." (as in, "I wasn't able to do it on my own, so God..."). To illustrate, here is a story from Amy Carmichael, missionary to India. Midway through her ministry, she suffered a terrible fall and was bedridden for the final twenty years of her life. She wrote to a friend, "A day or two ago when everything was feeling more than usually impossible, I opened on Psalm 40... 'He hath put a new song in my mouth, even praise.' How like Him it is to 'put' it there. We couldn't find it ourselves so He put it. And when He puts it we can sing it." (*Candles in the Dark*)[6].

The psalms are meant to be sung, and God helps us sing them from both our pain and our joy. For those of us who mourn, songs are a perfect way to praise him for being with us. It may be only a quiet hum of gratitude for his daily doses of mercy and protection. But however it comes—much like laughter—it lifts our hearts and releases great blossoming hope in our God who loves us. And with this fragrant blossoming, our hearts will do at least a tiny hand-spring of joy, if not yet a full-scale leap. So let's sing to Jesus! Let him put a new song in our mouths!

We can sing alone in our kitchens fixing breakfast, or with the big blessed crowd at church. Sing in the woods with

---

6   Taken from *Candles in the Dark* by Amy Carmichael. Copyright 1982 by Amy Carmichael. Used by permission of CLC Publications.

the sparrows or in the car on the way to the store. I've heard it said that when we sing, we pray twice, so though I can't sing well, I try to do it often. Songs can express what our hearts feel but have trouble articulating. When we sing, healing memories and tears may surface, or perhaps even buried thoughts and experiences that need attention. All these "joggings" can aid in our hard work of moving through grief.

Be blessed also by the knowledge that our Father sings us a lullaby each night. It's his love song over us, to soothe and deliver us out of our pain, as he watches us sleep. He does this because he loves us so much.

Dear Holy Spirit, I'll bet you often finish our tortured prayers ("… when we don't know what we ought to pray for…") by singing a praise song to Jesus. Thank you for reminding us of the blessing of singing, and help us to hear, in every note we raise, your promise of a stronger heart—a heart that hopes in you.

Print the word "SING!" on small cards and place them in your kitchen and bathroom and car, as reminders of the benefit and sweet blessing of singing to Jesus.

29

Hope

We wait in hope for the LORD;
he is our help and our shield.
In him our hearts rejoice,
for we trust in his holy name.
May your unfailing love be with us, LORD,
even as we put our hope in you.
PSALM 33:20-22

Hope is—in the world of Emily Dickinson—"the thing with feathers that perches in the soul." Hope knows, believes, expects, never fails. But when all hope seems gone, what is left? We hoped our children would be protected, and kept safe... that they would always be with us and have long happy lives. Now those hopes have vanished, and what has replaced them— grief, bitterness, loneliness and disappointment. Not a great trade-off, is it?

Do you feel that your life is over because your child is no longer here? I often have that feeling too. But then I notice that I'm still living and sometimes able to laugh and sing, which tells me that evidently my story has not ended. Instead, we are promised more blessings, more wonders, more songs and more love. So we ask Jesus to help us remember the rest of the story—that though his followers were crushed in grief at the cross, each of their lives continued in new hope and victory. Therefore we ask you, Jesus, to please help us trust that everything you allow, including this grief, has a purpose. And this is our great hope, that you will triumph over evil, renew broken hearts, and replace all we have lost—that your plan will come to pass. Let's trust in that blessing. It may not happen in our lifetime, but Jesus will keep his promise.

As we wait for all things to become right, we will be amazed to experience his love in new ways. We will learn that his plans are not to devastate us, but to bring us to stronger faith in him. The little bird that perches in our soul sings sweetest "in the gale" and "in the chillest land." That is surely where we are now, but it's also where hope is—hope in a faithful God who guides and shields us. So we watch and wait, and together we learn that our Father is good and his ways are higher than ours, often beyond our understanding. But he never makes mistakes or withdraws his love. Instead, he is creating something new and good from our pain. So we pin our hopes on him, and choose to trust that a new world waits on the other side of grief. We have hope for the future, knowing he will carry us. The little bird may fly off, but will soon return to be shared with others. This hope keeps many warm, and this is not the end of our story.

Dear Jesus, you are our only hope. Even though we don't understand, and the pain is unbearable and you seem so far away, we could not leave you. LORD, where would we go? With your blessing of hope, our loss has meaning, and we will survive. Amen.

Where are you now in this journey of grief? Looking back, is there a particular stage or awareness that helped you find renewed hope?

𝒯rust

*Those who know your name trust in you,
for you, LORD, have never forsaken those who seek you.*
PSALM 9:10

Birds are special to our family, so it might not be coincidental
that on the heels of the "Hope" bird, "Trust" brings another.
This one appeared some months after Sara left us. My husband
called as he was weeding in the yard, and I realized he was in
the same spot where, before her illness, Sara had sat with him,
pulling weeds and talking. But this day brought a different
visitor. At my husband's feet, scratching in the dirt, was a small
gray dove. "She just flew in and has been here a while," he said.
"Go get some seed and see if she'll eat." The visit continued
as we sat like dumbfounded children, while the dove perched
on my husband's shoulder, scratched in my hair and even ate
from my palm. Like many of us, she was happy with just a few
crumbs of love. As dusk approached, we started for the house
and the little bird flew along with us, as if to come inside. But
at the door she turned and veered off towards the sunset, and
we never saw her again. But we were reminded of Noah's dove,
who returned to him when the flood receded, and how the Holy
Spirit, as a dove, visited Jesus at his baptism. And we wondered
if this gentle symbol of peace was sent as reassurance that our
daughter is safe and happy—that God has kept his promise,
and that we can trust him.

We peer into the unknown, seeking answers, because
in this bleak place our hearts are trying to trust God. Despite
the fear and doubt this grief brings, we find there is only one
remedy—that is, to take a heaping dose of God's story every
day. In it we find our lives mirrored—broken and sorrowing
but healing and hopeful, never forsaken. His Word is our
only cure, with answers and promises we desperately need,
especially his promise that we can trust him. He will always be
with us. Because we know his name, when we call he answers,

sometimes in unexpected ways, as he did with our little dove. And with each response, our trust grows stronger. When we look back at history, we see him faithfully protecting, preparing and providing for his people. So we need not fear when we look ahead. He is still here and he will not forsake us.

This is where I am now—shielded by the LORD, sustained and unafraid. With the blessing of trust comes the best news of all: our children are not lost, only separated from us temporarily. They're with him, and if we stay close by his side, that is where we also will be one day. This I choose to believe, as I look forward to a day like no other. So we continue to call on Jesus and take his promises seriously. He will make all things right and we can trust him with our children. And then in this quiet trusting there emerges the most precious blessing of all—our hearts fall in love with him.

My Jesus, please send your Holy Spirit to our confused minds so we can grasp the truth of your faithfulness. Even when we don't understand you, we choose to trust you. Please comfort our hearts and be our Beloved.

Are there other experiences, aside from your child's departure, which may be keeping you from trusting? If you wish, write about disappointments that have hindered your trust in God. Compose a prayer asking Jesus to heal these wounds and open your heart to your loving Father.

31

Love

I love the LORD, for he heard my voice; he heard my cry for mercy.
Because he turned his ear to me, I will call on him as long as I live.
PSALM 116:1-2

Can you picture this? In your grief you cry out and God turns
his ear to you! That's spectacular, if you let your mind envision
the scene. He turns, hears and showers us with merciful
blessings. That's why we keep calling, because we know he can
be trusted to make his love real to us in our grief. And we learn
to love him in return. Love and trust need each other in order
for both to become real. It's this way in all our relationships,
but most blessed when it comes to God and grief. We mothers
who have given up our children are some of the most vulnerable
of all his creatures, and our wounds appear fatal. Each torn
heart string, each brutal blow, each soul-piercing cry connects
us to him. And in his compassion, he weeps with us. So we can
say with full voice, "My flesh and my heart may fail, but God
is… my portion forever" (Psalm 73:26).

But wait, there's more! In *Just Like Jesus*, author Max
Lucado writes:[7] "God loves you just the way you are, but
He refuses to leave you that way. He wants you to be just
like Jesus." What a daunting notion, in the face of all our
challenges! Be just like him? Daunting, yes, but impossible?
No. It boils down to one simple word—love. Jesus says we'll
love like him when we become more mindful, more open,
more forgiving and more generous. This is how he loves, and
in his Word he gives countless examples of what these "love
qualities" look like, showing they are do-able. After choosing
the twelve apostles—those he picked to be most "like" him—
he gave his favorite teaching, the Beatitudes, which is all about
love. Like those twelve men, we are his blessed followers. With
our hearts attuned to his, we can love like and for him, and
find happiness with him, apart from our circumstances. In this,

---

7   Taken from *Just Like Jesus* by Max Lucado. Copyright 2008 by Max Lucado. Used by
     permission of Thomas Nelson. www.thomasnelson.com.

we realize that love is not something we do; it's something we are, our true selves.

Our love relationship with God is like a well-watered, fragrant garden that attracts visitors. Our role is to surrender as streams of his divine love in the world, thereby growing our faith. As we grow, we bring others into the garden, where he can love them as well. And in our surrender, the Holy Spirit shows us that our children are not really gone because they live in that love. As long as we keep them close—in our thoughts, words and traditions—they will always live. As an example of holding her child close, Melanie's mother recently shared a photo of a simple wooden sign-post set up by her family along a lane on their ranch, inscribed "Melanie's Path." It was here she often walked—now a sweet reflection of their love for her. Like Melanie's mom, I don't want to leave my girls behind, but instead find ways to hold onto our love and keep them connected to my life today. For love is timeless and never ceases to exist. And our grief is never really "over," because there's no such thing as good-bye.

Psalm 86:13 says "Great is your love toward me." Dear Jesus, we are blessed that you love us "warts and all." As we struggle through our daily routines, help us to grasp the reality that we are known and loved by our great God. As we hold this truth to our hearts, you cheer us on and we love you in return.

Read the Beatitudes (Matthew 5:1-12). In grief, do you see yourself as "blessed"? How are you becoming more like Jesus?

$\mathcal{F}aith$

My eyes will be on the faithful in the land,
that they may dwell with me;
the one whose walk is blameless will minister to me.
PSALM 101:6

From trust and love comes faith. And even though we may love and trust Jesus, faith requires a personal encounter with him, like the one Mary Magdalene had at the tomb. There, she was the first to see the resurrected Christ, but her grief prevented her from recognizing him until he spoke her name. From the terrible beginning of our grief journey, every step has offered the same personal encounter, the same opportunity to meet Jesus face-to-face in our suffering, and his. He speaks our name and soon we realize that on this extraordinary journey, we are being gifted with the blessing of extraordinary faith. We are becoming the faithful in the land.

As a child I had very little trust and only a tiny mustard-seed of faith. Often my hectic upbringing left me frightened and alone, so I'd sit for hours in front of the glowing candles in our little village church, seeking to trust something unseen. However, the first glimmer of faith in God occurred one morning after an uncomfortable night with a neighbor family. I left before dawn to walk the few blocks over the hill to the safety of our house. I reached the crest just as the sun rose above the green valley before me, where an enormous rainbow flung its colors across the sky. I stood transfixed as God's gentle beauty broke through my fear, and I suddenly knew that he was caring for me and life would get better.

We grieving mothers can believe this today. God is caring for us and life will get better. But only as we trust him through the fires of adversity will we have faith that can stand. This is a huge test because in faith we are asked to be "sure of what we hope for and certain of what we do not see" (Hebrews 11:1). Doubt leads to unbelief, but faith believes without doubt that Jesus has saved us, is truly alive in us and calls us to serve him. All else rests on this; it is the means of our survival and the foundation of our spiritual life. Without faith, we are empty vessels. We have nothing.

Jesus offers us the blessing of faith so we can dwell with him. When Mary recognized Jesus, she fell at his feet in worship and he charged her with taking the good news of his resurrection to the disciples. Just as Jesus gave that privilege to a woman, he trusts us mothers to believe and be news-bearers. Of all the places we might place our faith, only faith in Jesus satisfies and saves us, because that's how we've been designed. Hear the words of St. Augustine: "You have made us for yourself, O LORD, and our heart is restless until it rests in you."

Dear Jesus, we come to deeper faith as we meet you in our grief, and trust that your will for our life is perfect. As in nature, faith grows like a tree if nourished and pruned. Thank you for helping our faith to blossom.

List your reasons for placing your faith in Jesus. What does being "faithful" mean to you? Is the Holy Spirit urging you to dwell with him, to honor him in your life? How will you respond?

33

Nature

The heavens declare the glory of God;
the skies proclaim the work of his hands.
PSALM 19:1

For my cousin Mary Ann, this psalm is a special part of her little boy's story. "It was a warm, sunny day in early August. My older children had been dropped at the public pool by their uncle. Matthew, my toddler, was too young for the pool but went along for the ride. On the way home tragedy struck. A door had been left open, and Matthew fell out and was fatally injured. The suddenness of this event left all of us in shocked disbelief. Friends and family gathered. Food appeared. We were stunned. As evening approached, Dad gathered the kids and took them outside to see the sky. He seemed to know that the answer would be there, in God's creation. Overhead, in a panorama of beautiful colors and rays flowing from the heavens, God assured us that everything was okay, that Matthew was okay."

"Obviously, the grief of that loss has never left our family. Tears are shed at every holiday and family event, as we remember Matthew. But our comfort and encouragement comes in knowing that we live in God's hands and that his will is perfect. Recently my son Joe told me that the events of that evening, nearly 50 years ago, are the source of his deep faith in God today. That is Matthew's legacy, his blessing."

In this tender memory we see once again that God is mindful of us and has a perfect purpose for each life. We watch the seasons change right on schedule, and realize that in God's amazing plan, he brings us Home in his exact timing. And we remember that he who holds the stars in place and the planets in their orbits is holding us, too—and in his hands we find assurance and comfort, especially when all seems lost. So let's go out and look up, just as Matthew's family did on that sad night. Let's set our minds on things above, things eternal rather than earthly. And as we think of heaven and our children, there's comfort in knowing where our hearts are—that they are set on God. He made the natural world as a reminder of his extravagant love for us. He's our good Father and his heart is set on us.

Dear Creator God, remind us to look up as often as possible, even when it's raining. When we see the moon, remind us that it's a reflection of the sun, and the sun is a reflection of your glory, as we also are. This is our faith, that we were created to reflect you to the world, especially in our darkest night. Thank you, Father.

Compose a prayer of gratitude to your Creator for a specific part of nature where you find comfort. Write it here, if you wish. How can you plan for more frequent time in nature? Do you need a dog to walk or a friend to join you? Will you go out and look up, and let God speak to you?

34

Stories

*Give thanks to the LORD,
for he is good; his love endures forever.
Let the redeemed of the LORD tell their story—
those he redeemed from the hand of the foe,
those he gathered from the lands,
from east and west, from north and south.*
PSALM 107:1-3

"Mama, tell me a story!" This familiar ploy is often used by children to delay bedtime, but it's a plea which echoes a need we all have to hear something wonderful, some good news. Those bedtime stories are like a soothing warm bath that calm children, give them hopeful thoughts, and prepare them for rest and another day. For us, the best stories are found in Scripture, gathering us to our Savior and his healing, especially now in our grief. We also find encouragement in the stories of those who Jesus has brought to himself, the testimonies of the redeemed. This was especially true in the life of my daughter Robin, whose love for the LORD prompted her to share him with everyone she met! Thankfully, she practiced on me, as the most persistent "agitator" for my conversion. She always began with a simple question, "Who is Jesus to you?" We heard the results of her prodding in the tributes of many friends at her memorial service. Their stories told of entire families finding Jesus as a result of that one question.

Blessings can be found and given in both the hearing and telling of stories. After Sara left, my heart was in pain over my two grandchildren, now motherless at ages 8 and 12. I wanted desperately to tell them stories about their mom. But because we didn't live nearby, I decided to make a book for them with stories of Sara as a girl, before they knew her. Her siblings and I wrote out our memories—often humorous—in a big scrap book with photos, mementos and Bible verses, and gave it to Sara's children. This act of story-telling has hopefully been a comfort and connection for them, but for those of us who wrote, the experience was very blessed, allowing us to pour out our love for this amazing person of ours.

So we'll keep those stories coming, especially the ones of our redemption! We'll fill our heads and hearts with these blessings—of how Jesus found the perfect way to gather us in and save our lives. We'll let his stories lift our heads, give us courage and grow our faith. And as we tell them, we pray that they will become part of someone else's survival guide. In the telling and the hearing, we will all find strength.

You, Dearest Jesus, are the great story-teller. With sweet parables, thrilling tales of action and bravery, startling examples of love and mercy, you have redeemed us! Please send people into our lives with stories of your goodness, to keep us connected to you. And in return, we will speak of your blessings.

Is there someone who needs to hear your story, for encouragement and peace? Or might it help your own healing to write to your child who is no longer here, with stories of your gratitude and love?

35

Strength

Be strong and take heart,
all you who hope in the LORD.
PSALM 31:24

...for he knows how we are formed,
he remembers that we are dust.
PSALM 103:14

Your hands made me and formed me;
give me understanding to learn your commands.
PSALM 119:73

The clay lump is cool and soft under my hands as I knead it, visualizing its eventual form. It began as a sack of clay dust, to which we added water. Now I'm "wedging" the lump by squeezing, pounding and throwing it until it's solid, firm and pliable. As I mold the clay, the shape emerges. I wrap it protectively, feeling love and pride for this unique pot I've created. It must dry slowly, or it will shrink too fast and crack. So I wait and check it each day, carefully holding it up to my cheek to feel its readiness. Then at the right time there's one last smoothing before it's fired in the kiln. Then a second firing, when a coat of glaze is applied. This is the beauty part, where the pot becomes its special self, with color and shine. Firing also makes it water-proof so it can be filled without seeping or falling apart. It is useful for pouring, holding or serving. This strong, unique creation is mine and it speaks of my gifts.

In the hands of God who is the Master Potter, we begin this way, as dust to which he adds life-giving water. The water may be tears of grief or the sweat of hard work. In his mind, our form and use are already planned. So he gives us the perfect life situation where we can experience the pressures and smoothing that will make us his, a beautiful container for his love. At the right time, in painfully hot circumstances, he allows us to be transformed into the unique, precious vessel he envisions and can use. He stays with us in the fiery furnace, as he did with Daniel's friends (Daniel 3). He blesses us with strength in the fire, as when gold is refined in a smelter or bread becomes useful in the oven—and most glorious of all, as when Jesus emerged victorious from the tomb, overcoming death and winning our eternal life.

Psalm 63:8 says, "I cling to you; your right hand upholds me." That is truly what he has done for us with his strong right hand. Throughout the earthquakes in our lives we can take heart because God upholds us, making us stronger than we ever thought possible. Most amazing is the knowledge that we have what others need; we can be used. We are treasures in jars of clay, because he has formed and fired us well. Then he pours in the holy oil of his love, which we in turn pour out on others. We are his workmanship which he prepared before the beginning of time for his good works. And in his strength, we become his vessels.

O Jesus, we thank you for all the ways you've used your hands to create the universe, part the sea, heal the sick, and multiply loaves. Then, those hands were outstretched on a cross and pierced with Roman spikes for our salvation. Please stay with us in the furnace—make us strong, with courage to serve you.

What have been your strengths during this season of grief? In what area do you need God's strength today? Compose a prayer to thank Jesus for the ways he has helped you survive and be filled.

36

Courage

You, LORD, hear the desire of the afflicted;
you encourage them, and you listen to their cry...
PSALM 10:17

God is our refuge and strength,
an ever-present help in trouble.
Therefore we will not fear,
though the earth give way...
PSALM 46:1-2

It's no secret that when a child leaves this earth, the mother
needs an enormous amount of encouragement—or literally, to
be given courage. For the mother of a terminally ill child, extra
doses are needed because, in caring for him or her, grief arrives
early. This is my story which I know echoes the experience of so
many of you who sat at the bedside, alone and afraid. Robin's
cancer was slow-growing and terminal for quite a while, but
on the day of her phone call, the earth did give way and my
grief began in earnest. She asked me to come because she had
been placed on hospice, needing full-time care and she wanted
to remain at home. Robin lived alone in a city that was 1,800
miles away, but I arrived the next day. When my husband put
me on that plane, I was unaware that I was about to lay down
my life and would need huge doses of God's courage.

In Robin's situation—terminal cancer plus breathing
problems—I tearfully packed funeral clothes, expecting to
be gone only a few weeks. But God had other plans. Have
you noticed that he often gives us only what we can handle,
a little at a time? So began what I call "The Year of Living
Dangerously," because as Robin's caregiver, I was in constant
fear. First off, I'm a terrible nurse—too impatient and jumpy.
And Robin had become very obsessive-compulsive during years
of chemo and constant pain. So I was hit with a terrifying set of
challenges, including filling the oxygen tanks (scary), a round-
the-clock regimen of pills and morphine (exhausting), and

Robin's frequent outbursts. To witness her suffering up close took all the courage I could muster, and for that, I clung to my mind's image of Mary beneath the cross.

On most days my only prayer was "Jesus, help us." Making a mistake was my greatest fear, and God had me in a place of total dependence on him. The days lengthened into months, then a year, and it never got easier. But his ever-present help carried us through, and he mercifully made sure I never once lost my temper. Also, that full year was the perfect amount of time to heal and restore the many broken relationships in our lives. He was working the entire time and it was miraculous. He was our only courage.

At the end of that year he took my girl Home, and I understand life so differently now. Grief can either crush us or lead us to transformation in Christ. Only with his courage can we can face this trauma and fulfill his purpose for us. He gives us much more than a simple pat on the back or a feel-good pep talk. I was bolstered with reminders of God and Joshua crossing into the Promised Land with phrases like, "Wherever you send us, we will go," "I will be with you," and "Be strong and courageous." We can be confident, because God's courage shines, especially on those painful days. Pray for it.

Dear Jesus, we look at the cross where you laid down your life for us, and we are overwhelmed. We see only a shadow of the courage it took. Now, as we grieve for our children, we are helpless to face life, to trust, to be confident—but we know you hear our cry and with your courage, Lord, we can overcome.

List the ways God is providing courage for you to move through this grief. What have you found yourself doing or thinking that at first seemed impossible? How have these moments of courage given you confidence?

37

Confidence

I remain confident of this:
I will see the goodness of the LORD in the land of the living.
Wait for the LORD;
be strong and take heart and wait for the LORD.
PSALM 27:13-14

On that early morning in Robin's hospital room, when the
nurse said "She's gone," I imagined her slipping away to the
other side of a veil. In my mind, she was separated from me
by only a thin slice of air—and as she entered that space, she
was "taken unto" God. The Bible gives us this confidence when
it says that as Jesus was leaving this earth, he promised his
disciples he would come back for them and take them unto
himself. I believe that's what happens, that we are immediately
welcomed into the goodness of the LORD in the "land of the
living," and so are one with him everywhere, forever.

So I don't often use the usual words or phrases for death.
I prefer to think that my girls just left or are gone, and though
we may be separated physically, we are together in spirit. Their
earthly work is finished, but they are fully alive and happy
with him, as we also will be one day. We wait for this with
the confidence that Melanie's mother found in Psalm 27. She
explained, "I read it and it touched my heart, and that was the
day Melanie went on to live with our LORD."

My new neighbor and I were getting acquainted, as
she had just moved here from Hawaii. When I told her that
my daughter had once lived on Maui, she asked, "Where is
she now?" I replied without thinking, "With God." And
that's what I believe. She simply entered his kingdom, which
stretches from creation into eternity. As Sara's earthly life faded,
she whispered to me that she wasn't afraid and I knew that his
goodness and love followed her. She and her sister are now more
alive than ever. They have left us for only a little while—just
a temporary separation, almost like they're on vacation! With

Jesus! Maybe even surfing on the heavenly winds, which would suit Robin perfectly.

*Please rejoice with me—our children now dwell with him forever! Thank you, L*ORD*, for this confidence, a beautiful blessing which eases our grief and expands our understanding of who we are in you. Amen.*

Confidence in God is an essential ingredient in our faith. How has he proven himself in your life so far?

38

Understanding

Show me your ways, LORD, teach me your paths.
Guide me in your truth and teach me,
for you are God my Savior, and my hope is in you all day long.
PSALM 25:4-5

Think about this! Life is a classroom where truths are discovered, knowledge seeps in and we are tested. The Teacher explains, assists, demonstrates and provides tools and practice—lots of it! In child-grief, the Teacher must dole out very special instructions. Guided by his hands and heart, we come to know his ways and to trust him. But oh, there's still so much we don't understand. "Why are some lives cut short?" "Why a newborn baby, or even one stillborn… What's the good in that?" "How can this be a God-given blessing?" My daughters lived only half their earthly lives. Sara's two children can now barely remember her. "We don't understand, LORD!" We shake our fists and cry, "Why, LORD? What are you thinking? Show us your ways! Help us understand!"

Then one day God did show me something. I had tossed some pebbles into a pond and was watching as each one stirred up concentric circles—rippling out and merging with others as it grew. This lovely interaction reminded me of our lives and God's mysterious ways. I imagined the Teacher explaining that he tossed in each life for a specific purpose, and that all lives are equally valuable regardless of their size. Each one touches others to influence and generate new experiences both precious and needful, and the process continues forever. All beginnings and endings, in the perfect plan of God, create a blessed dance of life. Thus, we are all connected and no life is wasted. When a life ends here, it is complete, having fulfilled its purpose. But it isn't over—it flows on to the spiritual realm, where it continues with God.

Scripture shows us that God has always used tragedy to draw people in and to reveal himself. He wants us to know him well so we can embrace his ways and enjoy him forever. We read in his Word: "You make known to me the path of life; you will fill me with... eternal pleasures at your right hand" (Psalm 16:11). Get that word, "eternal?" That means "never-ending!" Our lives are not limited to these human bodies, but continue on in our souls and spirits, our eternal selves. So we study and listen and think, and slowly we begin to understand, to see anew. And when we stand in God's presence, we'll see even more clearly that he used tragedy, not as punishment, but to bring us and others to himself. We understand, we know him, and that gives us a special story to tell.

Triune God, we're learning to lean on you and to see with your eyes. There, our minds open, our hearts become tender and we long for you to begin a new work of love in us. May we come to know you so well that your love reaches all our world. In the name of Jesus we pray, amen.

Think of all he's teaching you in this grief, and invite him to teach you more. Can you trust him with your fears, questions, unbelief? Sit with him each day, imagine resting your head on his shoulder as you learn.

39

Telling Others

I do not hide your righteousness in my heart;
I speak of your faithfulness and your saving help.
I do not conceal your love and your faithfulness
from the great assembly.
PSALM 40:10

"Look! Have I got a deal for you! Let me tell you about it—it's incredible news that will change your life! You really must try this… you'll thank me for telling you!" Don't we love to share good news? When we find something amazing we rush to tell everyone, especially if they desperately need what it offers.

Psalm 40 turns our focus away from our grief and towards telling the great assembly about him and all we're learning. Our new understanding, forged of Christ's love and the Holy Spirit, urges us to share that he is enough, he's sufficient to meet our needs when the pit is deep and the suffering long. We become walking proof of his faithfulness— we become "comfort carriers" for him. We tell others, we witness. But it's not always easy.

Jill Briscoe's book *A Little Pot of Oil* speaks to our feelings of inadequacy when faced with the desire to witness. She writes,[8] "We expect God to pour in before we start pouring out… to pour in courage before we take action… to pour in strength and inspiration before we obey Him… but it doesn't work that way. We first have to be obedient to the Holy Spirit. The LORD doesn't say 'I will fill your mouth first and then open it, but open your mouth wide and then I will fill it.'"

Here we are assured that the Holy Spirit will nudge us when our story needs to be told. In opening our mouths, we're having church and communion together, anytime, anyplace. It's what happens when we share what Christ has done. Though we understand only a small portion of who Jesus is and does and gives, nevertheless we speak, shout, sing, or whisper, "He will

---

8   Taken from *A Little Pot of Oil* by Jill Briscoe. Copyright 2003 by Jill Briscoe. Used by permission of Penguin Random House.

save you! Come meet my Friend, Jesus. Run to him! Drag your poor, tattered heart to him. Or call out and he'll run to you. He will save you!"

Soon we find our prayers becoming less about us and our needs and more about following his way. These prayers are weather balloons, directing us to places in a storm where help is needed. In them we see Christ's desire for relationship—close, loving, active and authentic relationship with him and others. We become wounded healers, and for that he gives us wisdom, his tender heart and his Spirit. This is our main job, to go out and find others like us, to point them to Jesus, to bring him honor… and to help walk each other Home.

Dear Jesus, we're not sure how to help anyone, but you will open doors. As we bend to your will, please use us to tell others what you have done, and in this telling we will gain wisdom. Thank you.

How do we speak? Who can we touch? What can we offer? Encouragement—Kindness—Smiles —Prayers—Listening—Stories—Food—Friendship—Walks—Songs—Tears—Laughter—Hugs—Love

40

Wisdom

*Teach us to number our days,
that we may gain a heart of wisdom.*
PSALM 90:12

In this blessing we see how precious all of us grieving mothers are. As we experience each phase, we gain wisdom as valuable as pearls, which grow beautiful in the most difficult circumstances. Pearls are formed when a grain of sand slips into an oyster's shell. To protect itself from irritation, the oyster covers the uninvited visitor with layers of nacre, the substance that fashions the mollusk's hard exterior. Layers of nacre coat the intruding bit of sand until it becomes an iridescent gem. Isn't this the perfect description of how wisdom forms in us during grief? It's like a luminous pearl that grows as it protects us from an unwelcome invader.

Similarly, in the gray ugliness of life without our child, God's Word guides us. It then grows into wisdom as we learn his ways and how to live this new life with honor, awe and respect for him. Godly wisdom is found throughout the Bible—especially in the Book of Proverbs and the life of Jesus. There we are encouraged to use our gift of free will by making wise choices, and to love and help those who need us. Wisdom also asks that we not make grief our identity, but rather let it teach us who we really are in God's eyes. So that, in wisdom:

We who could be discouraged say
     "God is my strength."
We who could be angry say
     "God gives me understanding."
We who could be depressed say
     "God's creation lifts my spirit."
We who could be broken-hearted say
     "God is healing me."
We who could be lost say
     "Jesus is guiding me."

We who could be lonely say
      "Jesus is with me."
We who could be suffering say
      "God comforts me."
We who could be confused say,
      "The Holy Spirit is teaching me."

As difficult as it may be, let's try to see every day as precious—a day to be with Jesus and take him to others. Our sufferings lead us to look more deeply at how God works and to find greater appreciation in his wisdom and provision. As we respond to him, our own hearts become wise, open to all he is making of us. Wisdom shows us that the blessings we receive—even though they are not what we had hoped—are his best plan for us. With his gift of wisdom—even as tiny as a grain of sand—we are growing a relationship with him that will not simply survive, but thrive. And as we embrace that fact, we find contentment and gratitude waiting in the wings.

O Jesus, we don't always understand life and its unfairness, but you have shown yourself to be good. Please grant us wisdom to trust you for what we cannot see, along with hope to carry us through.

List changes in your emotions, understanding or reactions that show you're gaining God's wisdom. Do you recognize examples of "worldly" wisdom as opposed to the "Godly" variety? Care to write about some?

41

Contentment and Gratitude

I was pushed back and about to fall,
but the LORD helped me.
The LORD is my strength and my defense;
he has become my salvation.
PSALM 118:13-14

One of my best friends, June, is incredibly wise. She is also
the most kind, cheerful, contented and grateful person I know.
Years ago, as my high school art teacher, she helped guide
me into that profession. June is also a fine water-colorist, and
most of her gift is devoted to illustrations of Scripture verses
and other art work for her church. June has not had an easy
life, having mourned her son David for years and suffered
other losses. When I asked for her favorite psalm, she referred
instead to the following verses, saying she loves them all, but
these have been her major healers. Read them and hear June's
beautiful spirit sing.

Do not be anxious about anything, but in every situation,
by prayer and petition, with thanksgiving, present your
requests to God. And the peace of God, which transcends all
understanding, will guard your hearts and your minds in Christ
Jesus (Philippians 4:6-7).

I am not saying this because I am in need, for I have
learned to be content whatever the circumstances. I know what
it is to be in need, and I know what it is to have plenty. I have
learned the secret of being content in any and every situation,
whether well fed or hungry, whether living in plenty or in
want. I can do all this through him who gives me strength
(Philippians 4:11-13).

These writings of Paul proclaim that the secret to
finding peace after tragedy is to seek out contentment and
gratitude. But will our broken hearts cooperate? It seems
impossible... but God. There it is again, that brief explanation
of what works. The secret is in his strength, which he gives for

the asking. The psalm says he defends and saves us. With this help, gratitude and contentment are not out of reach.

But yes, it's quite a challenge to see good in our lives right now. Some may feel that embracing life again means letting go of our loved ones, but that's neither true nor necessary. In fact, we're encouraged to find the best ways to stay connected to our children (check out "Afterthoughts" in the back of this book). And to make gratitude lists, enjoy positive moments and plan new adventures. These lift our spirits like good medicine, and we need daily doses. June's lovely watercolors are a perfect example, as they display the joy she shares with others. When we begin to put on contentment and gratitude, we warm ourselves and those nearby, and that may be all we're called to do. Paul wrote his verses from prison, able to teach only through letters. He was no longer allowed to preach openly, but he knew that God was there and his plans are perfect.

Lord God, as we soothe our grief by focusing on gratitude and contentment, we find your quiet, peaceful spirit. You have a purpose in our suffering, and we become content when we see life from your point of view.

Our grief has given us a deeper insight into how God works, and greater gratitude for his loving care and provision. Which of his blessings during this difficult time do you appreciate most, and why? Do you have a "gratitude list?" What's on it? Simple pleasures? A warm kitten to hold? A friend's smile? Morning dew?

42

The Sovereignty of God

...I have made the Sovereign LORD my refuge;
I will tell of all your deeds.
PSALM 73:28

...for the world is mine, and all that is in it.
PSALM 50:12

Now we must brace ourselves! This is the greatest challenge of all—to accept the sovereignty of God and to trust the perfection of his ways. Wisdom says he is good and that we are his well-loved children. But it's a huge leap of faith to believe that all he allows is for our best good. He says, "As the heavens are higher than the earth, so are my ways higher than your ways and my thoughts than your thoughts" (Isaiah 55:9)." Accepting this concept is essential to our survival, even though it describes a gulf wider than the Grand Canyon Gorge.

Scripture helps us understand that God is Creator, Lover and Powerful Ruler. He is sovereign. He needs no one, but desires close intimacy with us. He wants us to know and love him as he knows and loves us, and he's designed each of our life experiences for that purpose. Our part is to realize that we own nothing, not even our children, and to trust that his will—what he has allowed—is a blessing. He's King of kings but he's not a far-off ruler who simply observes and judges. No, he's our Father who walks with us in all seasons—in snowfall, rainstorm and sunshine. His love grants us free will so we can choose him, not as automatons, but as thinking, rational beings who trust him. And we can say, "Thy will be done… not my will but yours." In surrendering to his will, we accept that what he allows is best. Yes, bad things happen to good people. This is a hard truth, and in this critical time of grief, the tide can shift. It can carry us out to sea, away from God, or it can throw us head-long into his merciful arms. That choice is ours.

We may ask, "God, if you're in control, how could you let this happen?" We can ask, but he owes us no explanation.

88

He not only knows the exact gale-force of our storm, but he joins us in it. Yes, he can calm rough seas, but he most often uses his power to bring us safely through—so he can crown us, his beloved ones, with his love and mercy. His sovereignty is the linchpin around which all the facets of grief revolve, and it's thrilling to catch even a tiny glimpse of his work.

So we say, "LORD, when we go down to the sea, your sovereignty is on full display—vast, constant and powerful. Waves crash, recede, and each one—like the Word breaking— leaves a blessing. Mere man, what are we? Great Father, who are you?" When I think of my baby girl in that raging water, I realize anew that God was there, in control. He completed his work in his excellent timing, just as he allowed his perfect Son to pay the price for our rescue. When our children walked into his light, they also were perfect—totally redeemed. And who knows what they were spared? Or what good will come from their leaving? Only God knows. He gives us Jesus and he gives our children back to us. The mind cannot accept this, but the heart and soul can and does. He gives them back! On that day when we stand with him, we'll worship with glad hearts and say, "Wow! How great you are! How perfect are your blessings. Thank you, LORD Jesus!"

When I accept Your sovereignty, LORD, I can give thanks in all things. "I don't pretend to understand Your… purposes, or why You allow such pain in my life. But I trust You, believe in You, and choose to rest in Your sovereignty." – Joni Eareckson Tada, A Spectacle of Glory[9]

Write a prayer of worship for God's sovereignty and love for you and your child. Repeat it often.

9   Taken from *A Spectacle of Glory* by Joni Eareckson Tada. Copyright 2016 by Joni Eareckson Tada. Used by permission of Zondervan. www.zondervan.com.

43

Worship

Shout for joy to the LORD, all the earth.
Worship the LORD with gladness;
come before him with joyful songs.
Know that the LORD is God.
It is he who made us, and we are his...
PSALM 100:1-3

Sunny worships apples. Catching their scent, he wiggles his tiny cocker-spaniel tail in anticipation. This is his version of shouting for joy. This furry creature of ours knows what's most important in his life, what he needs more than anything, what he totally depends on every day. He knows the worth of apples and if he could, he would gladly lift his voice in a song of praise for each sweet slice. For now, tail-wiggling is a good substitute.

We, however, are called to worship only God, and to worship him in all things. Yes, that's all things, even the hard ones. Grief can surely lead us to question if and how we can do that. What is the value of worship? Can we give it sincerely? How can we possibly be glad and joyful? Do we really believe God loves us? Can we trust that our lives, our losses, are part of his perfect plan for us? Exploring the blessings that lead to worship is a hard process. But as we acknowledge our desperate need for his love and see signs of his healing power, awareness of his worth will follow. It will bring us to the doorstep of worship ("worth-ship"). And unless we're still stuck in the mire of anger, fear or depression, we're beginning to honor God as sovereign—as our Creator, Eternal King, Redeemer, Father, and LORD. A friend writes, "We can't help ourselves, we have no choice—our spirits cry out in praise, our mouths must follow."

In the Bible, the angels worship God day and night. And for us humans, the Holy Spirit asks us to praise God in every way possible, at all times—in corporate worship, in the splendor of nature, or when a word from Scripture touches our pain and brings relief. We also worship with questions, as a sign of trust in his wisdom and power. Ultimately, if we can thank our sovereign God for the many blessings in this grief, we have become worshipers. Our focus has shifted from our earthly concerns to heaven's reality. We recognize God's worth, and just as Sunny knows his apples, we know God is all we need in order to be fed, whole, loved and blessed. By giving him first place in our lives, we realize that others are to be loved, but he alone is to be idolized. No one and nothing is worthy of our worship except God, and we join the angels in celebrating that fact. The truth is, God designed us to worship him. Sunny's adoration of apples is strange, but our worship of God is natural. It's in our DNA, propelling us into humility and ever closer relationship with him. He planned it that way and it's all he really wants of us. So shout for joy, worship him with gladness, we are his!

"Praise God, from whom all blessings flow; Praise Him, all creatures here below; Praise Him above, ye heavenly host: Praise Father, Son, and Holy Ghost."—The Doxology, Traditional Prayer

Notice your thoughts and feelings either during or after a period of worship. What changes in attitudes, concerns or self-talk do you experience? Can you feel him calling you closer to him?

44

Humility

*My heart is not proud, Lord,
my eyes are not haughty;
I do not concern myself with great matters
or things too wonderful for me.*
PSALM 131:1

Here we are, on our knees, humbled before the worth of God.
Humility says, "Without you, we can do nothing. We surely
can't manage this thing you've called us to—to live well this
life of grief, to love despite our pain—it's not possible without
your help." So we must give up and relinquish control, in the
face of our helplessness.

Grief has brought us here, leading us to seek, begin
to understand, love and worship Jesus, "a man of sorrows,
acquainted with grief." He shows his humility as he kneels
without pride to wash the disciples' feet, simply loving. Then
we witness his ultimate humility on the cross. We need these
examples because humility is the most challenging of all
virtues. It's something we weren't born with—it needs to be
learned. For this, grief is an excellent teacher, a great humbler.
Grief is the one big thing we can't do alone. The mother whose
child has left may find that, for the first time, she's not in
control. She needs Jesus to carry her.

Most days we manage very well, thank you—and pride,
the opposite of humility, keeps us from asking for help or
admitting a need. Pride is too much of us, too little of God
and others. But here on our knees, our perspective changes and
we realize we can't save ourselves—only God can do that. The
humility of grief removes our blinders, revealing that God is
the only certainty in our lives, and we give the reins to him.
An additional blessing of humility comes when we find how
to love others well and live with them in peace, kindness and
patience. Humility does not attack or defend. Instead, it makes
us more forgiving and accepting, with gentle hearts that reflect

Jesus. Humility saves us from self-pity, and best of all, it helps us heal. So we don't hesitate to say "I need help," "I was wrong," or "I'm sorry"—and we humbly welcome what Jesus has set before us. We ask him for strength to accept our life as it is with all its emotions, thoughts, persons and conditions. With his help, we can give up our need for control or approval. We can trust only him for our survival, security and contentment. This is our cup. Let our hearts welcome it.

Our Heavenly Father, your name is holy.
Be King of my life, my heart. I embrace your will
for me now and for all time. Amen.

List the new evidences of humility you recognize in your grief. How have you given up control? On a scale of one to ten (one being the easiest), how difficult is the idea of giving God control of your life? What does that mean to you? What does it look like?

45

Work

You have searched me, Lord, and you know me.
You know when I sit and when I rise;
you perceive my thoughts from afar.
You discern my going out and my lying down;
you are familiar with all my ways.
Before a word is on my tongue,
you, Lord, know it completely.
You hem me in behind and before,
and you lay your hand upon me.
Such knowledge is too wonderful for me,
too lofty for me to attain.
PSALM 139:1-6

Jesus knows all we've been through—our grief, our damaged mind- and heart-sets. He knows that trauma has rewired our brains, and we need help to adjust. He knows what we need. And we are reminded of Mary Magdalene, who stumbled to the tomb on that first Easter. Confused and dazed, she didn't recognize Jesus until he spoke her name, but he knew her and perceived her thoughts. Once she realized who he was, he helped her by giving her something to do. Mary's worship brought her to the tomb that morning. She wanted to cling to Jesus, but he sent her off with an important task, something he needed to get done. He laid his hand upon her, and he changed her life.

Jesus does the same for us when we go to him in faith and recognize him as Lord. He speaks our name and says, "Go tell the others." And like Mary, our humble worship of him opens our broken hearts to service that uses his power, not our own. Shortly after my girls left, my pastor asked me to lead a grief group at our church. This seemed an impossible task, and little did anyone know that those who participated—our sad little band huddled together—would profoundly share the love of Christ. He hemmed us in and laid his hand upon us. It was a holy blessing, and we knew we were doing God's work with and for each other.

So we get up and go out. We find others like us and offer our care. Somehow, because Jesus has called us, these actions soothe our brains and tell our subconscious that we're safe. For those who work full-time, it might help to take occasional breaks to write journal notes about your emotions and feelings. Writing can be an outlet which helps you return to work less burdened and better able to concentrate. Full-time work is a challenge requiring extra doses of his power. But be assured that others who see your courage are receiving a valuable message, so let them know about your power-source!

One reminder: we don't work or serve to be "right" with God. Only faith in him makes us right by placing us in his way. There we can be used in the work he has planned for us. Work is given as a blessing, and we can walk through the doors he opens because we've been gifted to serve. We mothers serve in special ways because we're natural helpers, attuned to the needs of others. Volunteer at a center that helps kids with their homework, and soon you'll find yourself feeling happier. And who knows where, in God's plan, this will lead. The stories from that first grief group provided incentive for this book, as a way to help other mothers.

Jesus, during these difficult days when we're tempted to shut ourselves away and give up on the world, please keep us striving to become more like you. Help us to see work as your assignment, including this hard task of working through grief. Thank you for searching and knowing us. We pray to follow you, amen.

In what ways is God nudging you to move outside your pain and share his love with others? Is there someone who would appreciate your help? Who has inspired you or set a good example of God-like service?

46

Following

He makes me to lie down in green pastures;
he leads me beside quiet waters,
he refreshes my soul.
He guides me along the right paths for his name's sake.
PSALM 23:2-3

Sometimes I wonder if God gave us this psalm as a bit of tongue-in-cheek. At first, comparing us to sheep seems like a "not too charitable" joke. But then we get it. Yes, in many ways we are lost sheep in need of a shepherd—especially now. We've been in a very dark, winding valley, where it would be easy for a lamb to lose its way. It could wander off into a deep ravine of despair or fall over the cliff of guilt and anger. It could seek to avoid pain by straying into false comfort zones. But the Shepherd leads and rescues, and we're safe if we follow him, become like him. Following Jesus, we find ourselves in a greener pasture, rested and safe.

Psalm 37:3 says "Trust in the LORD and do good." As we follow and trust Jesus, we move forward in our recovery, and our lives reflect his goodness. He restores our souls, our essential parts that have been so badly battered. He makes us into followers with hope—and when others notice, we tell the story of his care and leading.

Let's take a walk along the shore together. The fishing boats are docked, having toiled all night, and the men are busy mending their nets. Look, here comes Jesus, calling to them. And just like that, they drop their nets and follow! They are his first disciples. After he teaches them his ways, they'll return to their families and friends and share what they've received. For them, it is perhaps the beginning of change, of being "caught."

And today Jesus calls us, so we drop our nets of pride and self-pity, and walk with him, knowing he will save us. Just as he told his first followers that he would make them "fishers of men," this also is his amazing plan for us. That's how it

96

works. Standing in his shadow, we learn to think and act like him. We also let him work through the trials we can't handle on our own. He proves he is the God of impossible situations, and he does what no earthly being can do—he restores us. Receive and follow him! He's the light of the world, and whoever follows him will never walk in darkness but will have the light of life. We find inspiration in the deep faith of Joni Eareckson Tada, who has been paralyzed for years. In *A Spectacle of Glory*, she writes this about her relationship with Jesus:[10] "When people see genuine, unfeigned optimism and a hopeful heart, they can't quite make sense of it or figure it out. I want to be Your ambassador just by staying encouraged, keeping my spirit bright, and maintaining a thankful heart."

Good Shepherd, please keep us close, especially in this valley of death and shadow, where it's so hard to see you. But you call us by name so we hear and follow. Please protect us, especially when our memories cause pain. Please remind us that we are being made holy.

Does the earthly life of Jesus inspire you to move outside your comfort zone and follow his way? Give some examples. What evidence do you see that the LORD is restoring your soul?

10 Taken from *A Spectacle of Glory* by Joni Eareckson Tada. Copyright 2016 by Joni Eareckson Tada. Used by permission of Zondervan. www.zondervan.com.

47

Memories

You kept my eyes from closing;
I was too troubled to speak.
I thought about the former days, the years of long ago;
I remembered my songs in the night...
PSALM 77:4-6

Memories can arrive as welcome guests or painful tormentors.
Or like mine—a mixture of both. They flood in when we look
at photos, hear a certain song or read a favorite verse. Other
times they come painfully out of the blue, barging in uninvited.
Memories can blind-side us at the arrival of a birthday or other
milestone, firing up mixed explosions of happiness, gratitude,
intense longing and sorrow. Whenever they wish, memories
visit and bring tears, smiles or surprise. Maybe even a good
laugh. Just be sure to hang onto them fiercely. They remind us
who we are and where we've been, and we need that.

Most urgently, God encourages us to think of him and
all his blessings of the past. One of my best memories of my
mom is her frequent bestowal of "God bless you," whether we
had just sneezed or not. She seemed so eager to say God's name
out loud, pointing us to him with that simple comfort. The
psalmist says, "I remember the days of long ago; I meditate on
all your works and consider what your hands have done" (Psalm
143:5). Look back, remember—and in those memories, see
and acknowledge God's love for you and yours, through past
generations. By remembering and being grateful for God's
guidance in former years, we gain courage for the future—and
we can sing in the night.

All our memories are blessings, precious gifts from
God given with loving-kindness and tender mercies. So when
memories come knocking, welcome them and all the emotions
that tag along. We can gently hold those pieces of our lives, even
amidst tears. Be creative; write a journal or make a scrapbook
about your life with your child or write a letter to him or her,

expressing things you never got to say. One mother I know has a party to celebrate her son's birthday, where friends enjoy memories of their happy times with him. Shared memories keep your child with you, and this is how healing begins.

Remind, O Remind O Remind, Dear LORD!
  With memories that speak to my heart,
Of laughter and love long ago,
  when I held their soft hands in mine.
Dear little girls, stay close—
  I need your sweet songs in the night.
Be not far from my longings,
  be not far from my heart.

Thank You, Father, for placing memories of
_____ *in my heart, memories*
that are precious and necessary to preserve, like flowers pressed
in a book. They remind me of my child's life and of all your
blessings that have enriched my days and turned me to you.

What ways have you found to celebrate your child's memories?

48

Healing

He heals the brokenhearted and binds up their wounds.
PSALM 147:3

*I will exalt you, LORD, for you lifted me out of the depths
and did not let my enemies gloat over me.
LORD my God, I called to you for help,
and you healed me.*
PSALM 30:1-2

Now, as seasons pass, we're stronger. God, not time, is healing
us slowly, in stages. He is lifting us and binding our wounds.
In grief, we've been crippled with pain, blinded by sorrow, sick
with longing and dead to happiness and hope. This is us. But
Jesus, our great physician, waits to heal us just as he healed the
blind, lame and sick who came to him 2,000 years ago. And
what does this healing, this binding up of wounds look like?
Because a mother's grief is unique, it leaves a deep scar that
never goes away. Instead, we learn to love it. It's a beautiful scar
which needn't be hidden. Those who urge us to "get over it"
don't understand—and we can't expect them to, unless they've
been here. Yet they speak in love, because it's hard for them to
see us in pain and they hope we'll return to our old selves. But
we never will.

Instead, God is taking us along a new path with a different
life view. His gifts of strength, wisdom, compassion and faith
are opening our eyes. Time is more valuable, relationships more
precious, and our actions more Christ-like. We make plans and
look ahead, and love and serve Jesus. Responding to his call for
compassionate action, we see that our grief journey is not merely
for our own transformation, but for the healing of the world. We
have been chosen for this, to be made anew, to love as Jesus loves
and to show what he can do.

Yes, our grief dims and we seem better, but it's never
gone. One friend said, "I think the healing part for me is
knowing that it's not going to go away, it's part of who I am.

100

And that's somehow comforting." Complete healing comes
only when our work here is finished and we join Jesus and our
children again. Until then, we stay connected. Our love for our
children doesn't leave because they do, so we keep them close—
we put their pictures up, talk to them, say their names out loud.
They're with us, so we honor them. Each mother finds her own
way, but the huge concept is that we're all connected, even after
this life, and that healing takes root when we follow God and
befriend his Holy Spirit.

*Jesus, our Healer, as you guide us through this dangerous
country of grief, your healing comes in many forms—as a strong
hand on our shoulder, comfort whispered in our ear and assurance
planted in our heart. You give us the Holy Spirit to pour the balm
of your goodness on us, LORD, and to renew our brokenness.*

How have you experienced the healing of Jesus so far?

49

The Holy Spirit

Create in me a pure heart, O God,
and renew a steadfast spirit within me.
Do not cast me from your presence
or take your Holy Spirit from me.
PSALM 51:10-11

Spirits seem mysterious, like ghostly beings that wander around
at night, but the truth is, we all have one. Our spirit is our
essential self with its memories, gifts and personality, which the
psalmist advises that we keep steadfast. That's a challenge for a
grieving mother whose spirit has been shattered. She needs God
in a special way in this new, sad, diminished life without her
child. And that's where the Holy Spirit steps in to help. We've
met him in Scripture as a dove, a tongue of fire and a burning
bush, and Jesus calls him "Comforter" and "Counselor." That's
because the Holy Spirit is the presence of Jesus, sustaining us
in our times of need. He encourages us, as we try to trust again
after so much loss. He knows our spirits are fragile treasures
to be held carefully. So he comforts us with reminders that our
children are safe and happy, with no more tears and no need for
us to worry about them. And that this separation is temporary
and we will be with them again. The idea that the Holy Spirit is
actually Jesus living within us is so profound that C. S. Lewis, in
Mere Christianity, was moved to exclaim, "… a first faint gleam of
Heaven is already inside you."[11]

As we struggle with our new, difficult life, we invite the
Holy Spirit in each day, because his blessings are essential to
our spiritual and physical health. He guides us in our prayers,
and I'm sure you've heard his "still, small voice" directing you
to Jesus and his truths, as you search. With his Spirit in us, we
are "in-Spired" with the gifts he distributes to each believer,
to be used for God's glory. Grieving mothers are gifted in an
unusual way, to create symbols of continuing love which can

11 Taken from *Mere Christianity* by C. S. Lewis. Copyright 1952 by C. S. Lewis. Used
by permission of Thomas Nelson. www.thomasnelson.com.

be passed on to so many others. One of their most natural blessings is that of helping and comforting.

The gifts of the Holy Spirit help us remember that our children's spirits still live, with all their memories and uniqueness. After my girls left, I was compelled to write a story about an orphan girl who lived in a tree house in her grandmother's back yard. It was titled *Sara Sunflower and the Still, Small Voice* and in it, this child was parented, comforted and saved by her friend, the Holy Spirit. He taught her, through many trials, how to live out the fruits of the Spirit—namely love, joy, peace, patience, kindness, goodness, faithfulness, gentleness, and self-control. The story's greatest value was to revive my mind and heart by giving me a child who loved the Holy Spirit. It also showed me that the Spirit of Jesus living in us makes our own spirits steadfast, held by his grace.

LORD Jesus, thank you for your Holy Spirit, our Counselor, Companion and Guide, to show us the way to you. We pray that you fill us with your Spirit each day so that our healing continues, as he makes us useful to you. In your name we pray, amen.

Have you begun to look on small miracles or realizations in your life as the work of the Holy Spirit rather than "coincidences?" List some here, if you wish.

How is the Holy Spirit prompting you, in your family, your church or community, to become a humble servant of others, to allow yourself to love more openly?

50

Grace

*Remember me, LORD, when you show favor to your people,
come to my aid when you save them...*
PSALM 106:4

Are you as surprised as I am that we've gotten this far? We
are surviving this journey of grief only by the grace or favor
of the Holy Spirit. I like what Anne Lamott writes:[12] "Grace
means suddenly you're in a different universe from the one
where you were stuck, and there was absolutely no way for
you to get there on your own." God's grace, his divine favor, is
usually unexpected, unexplained, miraculous, and given in dire
situations, in all shapes and sizes.

Grace. The word may evoke images of a Swan Lake
ballerina or a prayer before meals. But God's grace is something
that comes out of the blue, causing us to look back and say,
"What a surprise!"... "I never expected that!"... or just "Wow!"
Grace is the huge "But God..." and "Only God... ," and shows
up when we need a miracle, as I did during my year with Robin.
Stress seemed to be causing resentment to crowd out love for
my daughter, and I prayed and grieved over this constantly.
Then, one evening around Christmas, my God gave me the
most beautiful blessing of all. I was watching Robin—who had
been our star athlete, who embraced life with all the energy and
enthusiasm of an Olympian—now slowly shuffling her walker
into the bathroom. At that moment, I saw her anew as my dear,
frail, sick child, and my heart turned over. Intense maternal love
flooded my being, and as if she knew, she began sitting close by
me to watch TV. We even enjoyed a few rare laughs together. It
was the miraculous grace of God. We had prayed for physical
healing, but instead, his grace healed us differently. It was a year
of "grace upon grace" for my entire family.

Grief has been a long, difficult trek, searching for a life
without our child. Some of the early pain is behind us, and the

---

12   Taken from *Small Victories* by Anne Lamott. Copyright 2014 by Anne Lamott. Used
by permission of Penguin Random House.

mountaintop of acceptance may be within reach. Against all odds, we're surviving, and that's the surprise we didn't expect— that's grace. Our burdens are lighter, we see with new eyes, and possibilities appear in the hazy distance. In fact, we're being made new. I saw a recent interview with a woman after her grueling six-month hike of the Continental Divide. She said, "It was hard but I learned so much and my life is totally changed. I'm a different person." Doesn't that sound somewhat like our journey out of the pit of devastation? Grief continues (though much longer than six months). But he has come to our aid, he has favored and saved us and made us different.

In our grief, Jesus calls us to approach his throne of grace. In giving his life for us, he offered the most amazing grace of all—our salvation. Many of us have found Jesus for the first time in our suffering. We can trust him with our life, his grace-moments have carried us and we know we didn't blaze that trail alone. But what's ahead? What waits around the bend? Only God knows. Though we can't see the future, and many of the early terrors reappear, we know he's clearing the way. Wherever he leads, we can trust his grace to sustain us so we can pass it on to others. And we can look back on those unexpected, unexplained blessings and say "Yes, he has shown us favor. We are his people who have found him in our suffering, and his grace is leading us Home!"

Thank you, Father, for your transforming grace. Your blessings in the midst of our loss are convincing proof of your love. Your Word says that we are saved by grace alone, which may be the one source of joy we can experience in this life. For that we are grateful.

What is your story of grace? How has the Holy Spirit surprised you with this blessing in your grief?

51

Joy

You turned my wailing into dancing;
you removed my sackcloth and clothed me with joy,
that my heart may sing your praises and not be silent.
LORD, my God, I will praise you forever.
PSALM 30:11-12

With this psalm, my friend Patty writes about God's blessing in her child-grief. She says: "I didn't know Jesus when my baby boy died. But soon afterward, my husband picked up a New Testament from some trash at the side of the road, and as he read it, he turned his heart over to God. So I tried reading the Bible from the beginning, but I didn't understand anything. It took me another six years, during which time I attended Bible study and continued to search. Eventually Jesus did reveal himself to me, but through a book called *Clap Your Hands* by Larry Tomczak. After reading this book, I came upon Psalm 30:11-12 and my heart was touched. What a promise! I felt like I was alive again and my life and all its sadness was changing too. As time went on, my faith grew as I sought counseling and grief groups. But the grief is never really gone. It has been 49 years but it's still there."

Patty amazes me. In the years since her baby Gary returned Home, she has devoted herself to praising and honoring Jesus. After raising five other children, she and her husband took mission trips to Africa, helped get Bibles into China and now tell everyone they know how good the LORD has been to them. He definitely removed their sackcloth and clothed them with joy. They trust God's ways, even those that may not look or feel like they had hoped. Only he could transform their wailing into worship and fill them with joy— the joy of their salvation, the blessing of himself.

However, there's one big problem with expressing joy and happiness, and that's guilt. It's a favorite ploy of Satan the accuser, who tricks us into believing that any display of joy makes us seem unloving or disloyal to the memory of our child. But don't fall for that lie. God's wisdom allows us to experience more than one emotion at a time. We can feel joy mixed with sadness, or happiness mixed with pain. One does not discount the other, and mixed emotions don't mean we aren't grieving or we don't miss our child. They simply mean we're human. For many grieving mothers, it may take years for even a hint of joy to break through the extreme desolation of loss. But be patient. In God's grace, awareness of his presence can trigger a quiet leap of joy in our hearts, and that can be the beginning.

Then there's "rejoice," which means to have joy again. For the longest time I wondered if I could ever do that. In fact, I wasn't sure that joy had ever been a part of my life. Then I realized that joy means being thrilled, amazed and dumb-struck, which have all occurred frequently since I found Jesus. So now I still cry when I worship, but with joyful tears, tears of love. This is because grief has made one fact clear—there is great joy in surrendering to the will of God, and his salvation is priceless! When we have it, our sorrow turns to joy—a joy that shows others that we and our children belong to Christ. So we can rejoice, worship and sing his praises with tears on our cheeks and gratitude in our hearts for all his blessings, especially the joy of knowing his love.

But let all who take refuge in you be glad; let them ever sing for joy. Spread your protection over them, that those who love your name may rejoice in you (Psalm 5:11-12).

What does joy mean to you? What amazes you? Since your child left, are there ways God has moved in your life to bring you joy?

52

Acceptance

With God we will gain the victory,
and he will trample down our enemies.
PSALM 108:13

...we went through fire and water,
but you brought us to a place of abundance.
PSALM 66:12

Have you ever experienced the rare joy that comes with the successful completion of a New York Times crossword puzzle? If you have, you surely know there was supernatural help in this victory! In our grief experience, we face something similar to that challenging mix of unrelated words that are somehow connected. The phases of grief cannot be understood separately either. They are all bound together, each one dependent on the others. With God's help, we have moved through challenges, followed clues, connected the parts, and our life is beginning to make sense. And finally, after much trial and error, there emerges a beautiful solution—the victory of acceptance. We now see God, our children and ourselves as complete, intertwined and perfect, living our eternal lives here and now—under his protection, which continues forever.

However, we're still faced with the challenge of truly believing that his blessings are more valuable than anything or anyone on earth, including our children. Our desire to stay connected to them is healing, so we cherish memories, continue traditions, tell stories, and honor their values—and the bond remains. We will always miss them, but the truth is, our children are not really ours. In our new understanding of God and his sovereignty, we realize that he owns all and we own nothing, and as we take this truth into our hearts, acceptance comes. We release our children to him and rejoice that the Enemy has failed in his efforts to keep us in darkness and fear. And because God fortified us with amazing blessings, we have gained the victory. This is our great hope. This is acceptance.

Now with bravery and eagerness, we tell our story because we've been blessed with new wisdom, energy, compassion, and most of all, love. We joyfully accept the blessings of grief. The Father and Jesus have chosen us to share in their suffering, and in this, we have become rich. So in acceptance, we can say:

Yes, our all-knowing God chose us for a painful mission,
    and what he allowed in our lives has hurt us deeply.
We're not okay with what has happened, but our faith tells us
    that we are blessed with gifts of great value.
We trust this path that God laid out for us because
    his way is always toward life and wholeness.
Our good Father loves us unconditionally. His love is a coat
    of many colors to wear in joy as well as in grief.
Grief never ends, just changes. We don't stay there,
    but pass through it to carve out a new, meaningful life.
Grief isn't a sign of weakness, or lack of faith. It's the price
    of love, and in it, we keep our children close.
All events are stepping stones on our path to God.
    Ours is a grace-filled, blessed grief, binding us to Jesus.
We know the importance of our loss and can find
    the way forward. We are overcomers. We are his light.
He has given us abundance— a share in his work
    and a story with which to praise him.
And we can say, "This is my Beloved, my LORD.
    He has given me beauty for ashes."

Open your arms and your heart again to the world, for it has dealt you its worst and you are not destroyed! Fling wide the doors of your heart to the mysteries and blessings of life, for God can do all things and he grants you mercy and loves you with an everlasting love!—Carney and Long, Trusting God Again[13]

Afterthoughts

If you are reading this book because someone you care about is grieving for her child and you want to understand and support her through the pain, this section is for you. In it you'll find wisdom passed on from mothers who have experienced this exceptional trauma, because they want you to know how to help. First off, be aware that a grieving mother is super-sensitive to anything that sounds like advice or comparisons, especially if you haven't walked in her shoes. Don't try to explain her loss to her. Regardless of how well you know her, you can't possibly begin to understand her feelings at this time. Just know that your opinions are irrelevant right now. If you are a strong optimist, this process may be extra hard for you, but it can be done. Remember that the future is also irrelevant, so talking about "later," (as in "You'll feel better later" or "Everything will be okay") doesn't work. Instead, stay in the present or if your friend is talking about the past, join her there. Allow her to air all her feelings.

To show you really care, ask questions about her experience. Don't minimize any part of the story, even if you think her grief is out of proportion to the situation. Ask for details but don't try to cheer her up or give compliments. Instead, focus on her feelings. When she says, "This really hurts," say "Yes, it does." And remember that your comfort will be needed for a long time. In the early days of loss, the mother can be bombarded with condolences and visits and meals and flowers. But soon she's left on her own, at the exact time when her grief begins in earnest and she most needs support. So remind yourself that your friendship is still desperately needed after the funeral, when life has returned to "normal" for everyone else and she is in more pain than ever. This is when your compassion is most valuable.

Other ways to bless her:

- Pray ahead of time for the right words of encouragement.

- Ask about her child's life—special qualities, likes or activities, good memories, fun times, talents.

- Listen attentively, touch (hugs, etc.). Share your own memories of her child.

- Remember siblings with a card or special treat. They are hurting too.

- When the mother doesn't feel like talking, sit quietly with her.

- Call or visit regularly to listen, offer help, encourage or pray.

- Make contact on anniversaries, with no limit to years. Write a note with cards, flowers.

- Say or write her child's name. Try this: "I want you to know I remember ...." and use her child's name.

If you're afraid of saying the wrong thing, try this: "I'm not sure if this is the right thing to say, but ...." For added confidence, it may help to read "Friends" on page 45.

Here are things to never, ever say:

- "I understand how you feel—my dad just died."

- "Your child is in a better place."

- "Be grateful that you have/will have other children."

- "Well, it's really for the best."

- "You weren't ready to have another child yet anyway."

- "It was just her time to go."

- "His suffering is over."

- "It's time for you to move on."

- "Maybe God knows you can't handle children right now."

- "It's better to be married for a while before having kids anyway."

- "It's selfish for you to wish that she were back here on earth."

Important reminders: For grieving mothers it's a downhill slide and then an uphill climb. Recovery occurs slowly and inconsistently, rather than all at once. We all grieve differently and at different speeds. If your friend seems "stuck" in her grief, with intense pain that continues for years, you may suggest she see a grief counselor for extra support and coping skills. Grief groups are also useful, and fortunately, the internet makes it possible to connect with other grieving parents on websites such as:

Compassionate Friends (www.compassionatefriends.org) or GriefShare (www.griefshare.org).

You might also encourage or join her in a new hobby or activity that gives both of you pleasure and helps maintain physical activity, which is always beneficial.

Some friends avoid being with a grieving mother because they fear saying something that reminds her of her child. Yes, you may trigger a grief burst and release a flood of tears, but don't apologize or tell her not to cry. Instead, a warm gesture—taking her hand, hugging or patting—or even letting your own tears fall, if that happens—are ways to validate and share her pain. Most importantly, be yourself. Be the friend you've always been. A mother who's lost a child doesn't want to lose whatever she loves in you as well. That's what she needs most of all. Laugh. Cry. Be goofy. Take her to lunch. No matter what you read here, you can still be yourself.

For Moms: Suggestions for maintaining contact with your children who have left:

- Find ways to keep them in your life. It's what our spirits need—to continue the bond.

- Share stories and memories about their life whenever you have the opportunity.

- Start a project or join a cause they care about, in their honor.

- Watch their favorite movie or go to a place they love or always wanted to visit.

- Wear an item of clothing or jewelry that is theirs.

- Hold a meal gathering and ask everyone to share stories. Say a blessing in their honor, set an extra place.

- Make a quilt out of their tee shirts or baby blankets.

- Plant a daffodil bulb for each year they were with you, and add to the garden each year.

- Light a candle, display photos, speak their name, play their favorite music, serve their favorite meal.

- Write letters to them with family news. Say "I love you and miss you every day."

- Talk to them, keep things. (I treasure the lock of Sara's hair I've kept and I use Robin's Bible).

- Notice the times you're reminded of them. Write down the thoughts that come with these memories.

- Be creative—write poems and songs, paint pictures, design a garden—ask family members to contribute.

- Make a scrap book of memories, photos, messages, and memorabilia. Sit with it often and remember.

I sleep on her pillow, where there is less pain,
    And I see her small hand smooth the covers again.
There's comfort in knowing perfection is hers,
    And here in my heart she still laughs like a bird.
So we dance in my dreams, and sail far away
    To that place where she worships the Father today.

Acknowledgements

The abundant blessings of God helped write this book—
blessings in the form of many dear people who inspired, loved
and cheered me on. With huge gratitude I thank Lisa Weber
who is an amazing editor/advisor/encourager, David Bergsland
(http://bergsland.org), graphic designer and publisher
extraordinaire, and David's beautiful wife Patricia, who
graciously offered her painting for the cover.

I'm especially thankful to the mothers who so generously
shared their stories: Mary Ann, Patty, Cindy and June, and for
the prayers and encouragement of friends and family, notably
my best cheerleaders Jenny, Chris and Colin. Special love to
Teresa, Jeanie and Jim, Patty and Larry, Teena and Paul, Lara
and the women of the Hope Church Book Study, who have
prayed me through. I'm very grateful to author Jill Briscoe
(who lit the spark years ago), Mary A. Johnson (my very capable
mentor/reader), Yvonne Babbitt (whose "Thought for the Day"
ministry inspires and opens God's heart to me every morning),
and singer/songwriter Fernando Ortega (whose music always
honors Jesus and keeps me on track). And special thanks to my
mom, Betty, whose love never failed.

Michele, Kathy and John, Dee and Joy, you have been
such sweet memory-keepers for me, thank you. And Pat
Moss, you are the best husband and friend in the world, with
the strongest shoulders and softest heart. Your love gives me
courage. Mostly, all glory to our God, *tu, solo tu,* forever faithful.

Made in the USA
Middletown, DE
21 January 2021

31826579R10076